dance on!

Marcia Rudy

Copyright © 2020 by Marcia Rudy

All rights reserved. No part of this publication may be reproduced, stored in a retrieval system, or transmitted, in any form or by any means, electronic, mechanical, photocopying, recording, or otherwise, without the prior written permission of the publisher.

Printed in the United States of America.

Cataloging-in-Publication Data for this book is available from

the Library of Congress.

Rudy, Marcia
ISBN: 978-0-578-79246-0

10 9 8 7 6 5 4 3 2 1

CONTENTS

Raven Wilkinson 1

Violette Verdy 11

Juliet Seignious 19

Robert Maiorano 29

Carol Bryan 37

Marilyn K. Miller 41

Karole Armitage 49

Nanette Glushak 55

Francia Russell 61

Oleg Briansky 67

Gemze de Lappe 73

Ted Kivitt 81

Ann Reinking 89

Louis Johnson 97

Marcello Angelini 101

Candace Itow 109

Bruce Wells 113

Victoria Beller-Smith 117

CONTENTS

Photos 121
Gail Crisa 131
Rose-Marie Mene 135
David Fernandez 141
Donna Silva 145
William Whitener 149
Laura Young 153
Nina Novak 157
Amos Chalif 161
Daniel Duell 165
Darla Hoover 169
Bruce Marks 173
Peter Naumann 177
Lois Bewley 181
Colleen Neary 185
Frank Ohman 189
Hilda Morales 193
Delia Peters 197
Lawrence Rhodes 201
Michael Vernon 205
Photos 209

About the Author

Marcia Rudy is a writer as well as a former dancer and actress. She was born and raised in New York City, where she has written for many publications as well as for the theater.

When she was four, like most little girls for whom everything was beautiful at the ballet, she wanted to be a ballerina. But approaching adolescence, she quickly realized she was the wrong body type: flat feet, no arches, short torso. She transitioned to modern dance, studying with Eve Gentry, Hanya Holm, and at the New Dance Group, performing for several years in the New York City area.

For eight years she was a contributing writer for *Generations*, a newspaper focused on New York State's senior population, and found inspiration in the courage, determination and perseverance of her interview subjects (many of them in the entertainment and sports world). When *Generations* stopped publishing, Rudy decided to write "Dance On!" in order to continue writing in that vein. Ballet was an obvious topic, not only because of her strong dance background, but because of the special challenges ageing dancers face, precisely because ballet is so physically difficult and so beautiful.

Acknowledgements

Thank you to Aaron Kesselman for his extraordinary perseverance and contribution to editorial research, Bill Fallon for his unfailing support and encouragement, Grace Arden for her inspiring suggestions, and Anthony Parisi for his invaluable creative direction.

FOREWORD

The aim of this anthology is to explore how 37 ballet and classically-trained dancers, both retired and active, have dealt with the ageing process and their career transitions. I conducted these interviews over a period of time, roughly between 2007 and 2017. The dancers revealed how their self-perceptions evolved in response to the constraints or changes that ageing imposed upon them, and how they met those challenges along the way. A recurrent theme was how they had survived and continued to thrive in a culture, and an art form, that puts such a premium on youth and beauty.

There are those who worked diligently to keep their optimism and faith when confronted with the challenges of ageing, seeking new ways to negotiate their bodies. Others turned their focus outwards, seeking to foster attitudes of persistence and discipline in their students. In a few cases, the dancers sought new careers. Many, in interviews, expressed an interest in "setting the record straight" about things that happened in their careers, perhaps revealing a preoccupation with the past. Many gave credit for their success, in large part, to the unfailing support of their families and loved ones whose sacrifices allowed them to achieve their goals. Several were the first in their families to pursue a dance career. Despite a myriad of disappointments and frustrations, many said they would always think of themselves primarily as dancers. Some no longer did.

They are all inspiring.

Raven Wilkinson (1935 - 2018)

Making A Comeback

Sixty years after being turned away from an Atlanta hotel, African-American ballerina Raven Wilkinson returned to Atlanta, having been asked to speak to students in an elementary school. Many students had seen the film *Ballets Russes* and were very curious about Wilkinson's experience. "I wasn't planning to burst in and start talking to them about Atlanta," she said, "but once I was there I had to talk about it." Wilkinson opened up to the assembled students:

> You know something, about sixty years ago I was down at Peachtree Avenue at the Peachtree Hotel. I was going to dance at the Peachtree Theater that night, but I was put out, so I turned my back and walked away and went back to New York. And now I've come back. I never dreamed that sixty years later I would see all of you sitting here, the diversity—blacks, whites, Hispanics, Asians—a whole mass of people, all one and together, talking and sharing. It's like dreaming you would have a black president.

2   DANCE ON

But for Wilkinson, her early career was more like a nightmare. One illustrative example:

> It was the late 1950s, the middle of the afternoon. I don't remember what southern town we were in, there were so many. We were rehearsing a ballet called *Harold in Italy*. There were about 20 people onstage and we were in several groups. Suddenly, we heard all this shouting. We stopped and the piano stopped, and two men came running down the aisle. They were very rural looking, dressed in business suits, but talk about rednecks! I saw the backs of their necks and they were red—for real. The men stormed the stage, spitting terror. "Is this where the Ballet Russe de Monte Carlo is rehearsing? All right, which one of you is the *nigra*?"

Terrified, Wilkinson held her breath as one of the men shouted to the first group, "You all got a *nigra* in here?" Her voice became tense as she continued to relate the story. "I was in the second group. They asked us the same question and nobody answered them." She recalls standing there in the dimly-lit theater, trembling, hidden among the dancers. She knew the routine. Stay quiet. It was not the first time that the light-skinned Wilkinson had passed for white. The men made their way to the third group and again, everyone remained totally silent, just staring at them. The men's exit was less dramatic than their entrance: "finally," Wilkinson said, "they realized nobody was going to answer them and say, 'Here's the nigra!' so they went swaggering off the stage, back up the aisle, and right out of the theater. But they looked real proud of themselves."

The menace was real. "Everyone was aware that something could develop into an incident—you never knew what could happen, especially when you were dealing with people who were so hotheaded," she said. "These men could have had ranking positions in the theater, or they could have been policemen—they could have been anybody." Wilkinson gives credit to the entire company for protecting her: "All those people around me, they supported me so beautifully."

Similar scenarios were repeated many times. "It was a volatile time in the South," Wilkinson explained. "They had desegregated the schools in 1954. The South was beginning to realize they were going to have a fight on their hands because the federal government was suddenly telling them, 'you're going to have to get rid of this.'" Some states were worse than others: "North Carolina, South Carolina, Tennessee—we had to be very careful in those states. We tiptoed through them. Georgia, Alabama, Mississippi were difficult to the point where they could be downright dangerous." It seemed wherever she went in the South, people were lying in wait for her. "People took a terrible objection to the fact that there was a 'negro' ballerina in the company—they used the word 'negro' in those days."

In each Southern town, the routine was simple: Wilkinson's roommate, Eleanor D'Antuono, would stand on line at the check-in desk and get the room. Then Wilkinson would steal in quietly and join her there. The incident in Atlanta, in 1957, was the first time Wilkinson had been kicked out of a hotel because of her race. Sergei Denham, the company director, figured one of the bookers knew about Wilkinson, because by the time the company arrived in Atlanta word had spread. She was immediately recognized by the manager and told she would have to leave because this was a "white hotel." The manager said he would call a "colored" taxi and a "colored" hotel to see if they had room for Wilkinson. D'Antuono did not want her to go alone and was ready to leave with her, but was told she couldn't.

Wilkinson discovered that prejudice in the South wasn't just from whites but from blacks as well. "Because of how light-skinned I was, people were not always looking for it, although black people always seem to know," she said. She recalled a time when a hotel maid recognized her as being black:

> She was in the hall and was putting away some linens when I came out of the elevator. She was also black, and she just looked at me. I kept walking toward my room, unlocked the door and went to pull the curtains, leaving the door ajar. When I turned around to get the key, there she was, standing in front of me, hands on her hips as if I had no business being there.

Rather than take offense, Wilkinson engaged the maid in conversation. "I said innocently, 'Oh, maybe you can help me. Do you know a place around here where we can eat after the performance?'" As they continued to talk, the maid suddenly softened and said to her, "You are so beautiful—I saw your picture downstairs in the lobby." The exchange, and its lesson, have stuck with Wilkinson:

> It was so revelatory to me. I treated her normally, instead of responding to her abusive attitude, and as we talked we became very friendly. I went from someone she resented to someone she looked up to. She could be proud of me because I was her race. Here I was a black ballerina in a white ballet company.

Wilkinson recalls telling Denham before the company went on tour that if someone asked her if she was a "negro" she would not deny it. "That's like denying yourself as a human being and I just couldn't do that or go through life like that. If you do that, you start something you can't finish. It affects you, it affects your family, and it affects the people you are with in that moment."

One of the most disturbing memories for Wilkinson came in the '50s, when the company rolled into still another southern town and discovered they were in the midst of a Ku Klux Klan convention. There were families, adults and children, dressed in cloaks and hoods, running in the streets throwing pamphlets. Wilkinson made it into the hotel and went into the dining room to join the company for lunch. When she pulled out her chair to sit at the table, she noticed a neighboring chair piled high with cloaks and hoods. The demonstrators had taken a break for lunch and discarded their attire before they sat down. "Just like dirty laundry," she said. "I remember thinking, these people are nothing, this is all they have: to hate people, and they are teaching their children to do the same thing. All the white empowerment talk—it's just hot air." This was a turning point for the rest of her life.

Wilkinson's childhood in North Carolina was filled with the desire to perform. "Everywhere I went, if there was a stage, I wanted to get up on it," she said. That feeling never left her. She recalled being enraptured by her first ballet, at age five. "The Ballet Russe de Monte Carlo was dancing *Coppelia* at City Center in New York City. I saw Freddie Franklin dance the role of Franz and thought, 'Oh my God, this is magic.' I was hooked."

Her mother tried to enroll her in the School of American Ballet but was told she was too young, so she was enrolled in a school teaching a German movement system she described as a pre-Isadora Duncan form of natural inspiration. When she was nine, an uncle from California sent her money for ballet lessons as a birthday present. The gift occasioned a tour of all the major ballet schools in New York City. Wilkinson remembered being fascinated by Maria Swoboda, one of the great ballerinas with the Ballet Russe de Monte Carlo, who taught at the Ballet Russe School on West 54th St. Wilkinson joined in February, but because the class she joined had begun in September, she was given private lessons to catch up.

She vividly recalls her first lesson with Swoboda:

I was in shorts and sneakers, I stood there with my knobby little skinny legs, but Madame Swoboda was ready to teach me ballet. She showed me the five positions and corrected my arms and shoulders. She kept saying, "pull up, pull up." I got into first position, ready to plié, trembling with fear, and she asked me if I was French. I could barely answer. A little while later, she asked me if I was Spanish. I could barely answer that, too.

Wilkinson's mother thought that ballet was wonderful for posture and grace but wanted her daughter to have a normal school life. She attended Ethical Culture School in New York City on Manhattan's West Side and then went on to Ethical Culture Fieldston School in Riverdale, but was forced to change to Professional Children's School when she increased her ballet training to five times a week. By age 16 Wilkinson knew she wanted to become a professional dancer. She devoted herself to dance, sometimes taking two or three lessons a day.

Upon graduation, when she was unable to get into a ballet company right away, she enrolled in School of General Studies of Columbia University for two years while continuing to take ballet classes most of the day with Swoboda. In 1955, after her second year at Columbia, she left to join the Ballet Russe de Monte Carlo.

Through the years, Wilkinson has been compared to another stellar African-American dancer, Janet Collins, who auditioned for the Ballet Russe de Monte Carlo in 1934, in Los Angeles. Léonide Massine said he would take her, but she turned down the offer after Massine told her she would have to look "more white." The two never met, but Collins was an early influence on Wilkinson. "Watching her dance in *La Gioconda*, I saw what a passé could be," Wilkinson said. "She had such an extraordinary way of moving—piquant and light." Wilkinson added with a smile, "And they said a black woman could never dance en pointe."

Wilkinson remembers taking a ballet class at the old Metropolitan Opera House in New York City with Dame Alicia Markova and thinking that the great dancer had flagrantly ignored her, standing with her back to Wilkinson throughout the entire class, never commenting on her dancing, and never allowing their eyes to meet, even though Wilkinson danced all the combinations correctly. She quickly added, "Of course, I cannot be 100 percent sure that it was intentional. After all the prejudice I experienced in the South and all I'd been through, it could have just seemed that way to me."

After two years in the Ballet Russe de Monte Carlo, Wilkinson was forced to realize something her parents had always been afraid of: there was no future for a black dancer with an American company. She recalled the pivotal day, "I was rehearsing the third act of *Swan Lake* with Ballet Russe in New York City. The backers had come to see it. I was supposed to do the Spanish dance and I just assumed I was doing it. I had also been scheduled for *Les Sylphides*. When the time came, I was told that another dancer was going to do it. I just couldn't take anymore," she said. That night, she hid in the studio in which they had been rehearsing. The next morning, she ran away. After informing Denham she had to stop dancing, her director promised her parts in *Scheherazade* and *Raymonda*. But she couldn't help thinking the backers would get to him again, that she didn't stand a chance. "I was exhausted and I felt bereft," she said.

Wilkinson couldn't find another job in the dance world. "I don't know what made me think I'd be accepted by another company," she said. "I really lost sight of myself after that. I remember thinking, 'You have to accept reality.'"

Wilkinson had always taken refuge in her Episcopalian faith. "Whenever we were on tour, in my free time, I would always seek out a church to go into," she said. Now she joined a convent.

She reported being happy for eight months, until the day the sisters were offered tickets to see a performance of The National Ballet of Canada. Watching the dancers perform, she experienced the familiar pangs, that yearning to be on stage. Afterwards, she went backstage to say hello to an old friend whom she had known from the Ballet Russe. As they talked, the pangs became even stronger. Back at the convent, after sharing her feelings with the Reverend Mother, Wilkinson realized how much she missed the ballet. "In retrospect," she said, "maybe I should never have left. After all, nobody really knows why things happen in the theater."

She left the convent to return to the thing she loved most in the world, only to discover that America was still not ready for her. Determined to dance, she left the country to become a second soloist with the Dutch National Ballet. "Ballet dancers did not have the same problems with color in Europe," she said. She was happy there but missed the United States and in 1973, decided to return to New York City.

By then, things had changed. She was hired by New York City Opera, where she danced for ten years before gradually transitioning to acting, which she described as "still another satisfying career." Wilkinson enjoyed a nearly four decade run with the company until it met financial ruin and was forced to leave the New York State Theater. "When you've been in a place for 38 years, it's like home," she said. "It killed me to see City Opera close down." Her last work was in *Intermezzo* in 2010, the last production in which they hired actors.

Not many performers enjoy a career spanning six decades, yet Wilkinson still misses the theater. "I tell myself, 'You'd be a fool to let this get to you. You've had so many years of performing as a dancer and an actress.'" Having a career of such exceptional length has allowed Wilkinson reflected on the evolution of her artistry:

> I think the older you get, the more you absorb a kind of artistry in your being. You see yourself better as you get older. You develop emotionally and intellectually in a way you didn't when you were younger because you didn't have the life experiences to teach you. And so your artistic boundaries actually expand.

That expansion continues as Wilkinson accepts invitations to speak, teach and demonstrate in the New York area, including Dance Theatre of Harlem, the Brooklyn Friends School, and Fordham University. To witness her coaching the original choreography from the second movement of Ballet Russe's *Les Sylphides*, at the Westchester Ballet Center for the Performing Arts in Yorktown Heights, as I did, is to experience one of those rare moments when you are suddenly aware that you have witnessed something exceptional and significant that you will remember all your life.

Wilkinson may well have been the dancer best equipped to teach the original choreography of this great ballet. "Hands reaching out from the face, waving at the air, and at the last minute you turn your head," she said to about thirty youngsters from the intermediate and advanced classes, attending her master class. At 82, she seemed to have total recall of the choreography, without ever having jotted down a note. Her body seemed equally ageless. "I can still lift my right leg up close to my ear," she said.

Violette Verdy (1933 - 2016)

From Stage to Studio to Legend

When Violette Verdy, Distinguished Professor at Indiana University, prima ballerina and legend in her own time, was feted with the Jerome Robbins Award on Sept. 30, 2011, the dance blogger at Haglund's Heel wrote:

> Miss Verdy entered the stage with the authority of a dignitary and embraced the audience in grand style. When asked what was running through her mind at that time, she said, "I thought if I have one bow, I'd better make it good," and added laughing, "I was actually wearing a black dress a friend of mine had discarded."

Verdy had fond memories of that special night, when she stood in front of the audience along with 29 current and former NYCB ballerinas as part of the tribute to Robbins. "It was so nice to see everybody again." She recalled the experience of dancing for Robbins:

Jerry was without question on a quest for perfection. All artists have doubts, and in his case they were extreme, because in a way... I don't know how much success was important to him, but love was. Perfectionism was a way for him to reach out for love. He affected us all differently, but remembering the affection Balanchine had for him when he brought Jerry back to us helped us to understand him. Jerry and George—those two together were really something rare. You know, Balanchine told me that he, himself, was not really *the* American choreographer and that the great one was Jerry.

Reflecting on how her career began, Verdy recalled her childhood growing up in south Brittany, France, under German occupation during World War II. More than 70 years later, she had vivid memories of the soldiers everywhere, and that her uncles were in concentration camps. "I saw a lot of things...." Her voice trailed off as she remembered the horrors of the war.

No one in her family danced. Her mother was a school teacher. Her father had died young. She began ballet lessons at age nine, with Carlotta Zambelli, whom she described as the last of the great teachers from the Paris Opera. Of these early ballet classes during occupation she said, "It was a daring thing to do when we didn't have much to survive with."

While initially interested in music, she found she loved dancing more once she started ballet lessons. "I was a restless child. I was always jumping around," she said. The idea of making ballet a profession came gradually. She recalled being very shy but beginning to realize she was very good at ballet. She had a lot of turnout. She could do what her teachers wanted, and they were very encouraging. Ballet gave her something for herself—a personal freedom, something that she enjoyed amidst the harsh realities of WWII.

Her early promise was realized after the war with a meteoric career in France, which led to American tours and Verdy being invited to join American Ballet Theatre in 1957. When ABT temporarily disbanded in 1958, she was the only dancer invited to join NYCB. More than public adoration, it was always Balanchine's admiration Verdy sought. It was common knowledge that Balanchine wanted his dancers skinny, which suited Verdy's small frame. "It was the dancer's mission to show the discipline of the dancer over the body," she said. When asked to name her favorite partners she answered unhesitatingly, "All of them…for different reasons…Edward Villella, Jean-Pierre Bonnefoux, David Blair and Helgi Tomasson." Her favorite ballets? *Swan Lake* and *Giselle*, which she performed throughout the world, including with the Royal Ballet at Covent Garden and the Stuttgart and Munich Ballets.

After a 20-year career at NYCB she left to become artistic director of the Paris Opera Ballet, from 1977-1980, then directed the Boston Ballet until 1984 before leaving to head the ballet program at Indiana University's Jacobs School of Music.

As an educator, Verdy was able to pay forward the debt to her own teachers. "Everywhere I've been I've had incredible teachers: Russia, England, France, Canada and America, where I used to look in the yellow pages for the ones that said Russian Imperial," she said. But teaching also allows her to continue learning: "If you think you're a student when you're a teacher, you'll learn something about teaching every day," she said. Verdy is fond of quoting her favorite line in Rodgers and Hammerstein's *The King and I*: "By your pupils you'll be taught."

Verdy has grown to love teaching as much as performing. Her greatest challenge is that her students have had such different training, but like Balanchine, she looks to their individual qualities: "I cater to the limits and qualities of the dancers. Each dancer has a different personality. You cannot repress the individual personality."

Verdy has only the highest regard for her students. "They all come through the audition process on a very high level," she said. "They are incredible and they are very mature. You can speak to them directly," she said. "I can't believe they do what they do, and they don't have a moment to rest." Verdy, who studied both piano and violin before dancing and was celebrated for her musicality throughout her career, respects the fact that all her IU students also study piano. She explained, "Ballet teaches you etiquette, courtesy, and a high relationship between a woman and a man. It is very much because of the great music that we have; it is an elevating act."

She tries to give individual attention to each dancer, remembering the example of Balanchine in company class, five decades prior:

> Mr. B was always very patient with us. Sometimes he would see that we were not getting what he was after. I remember he would come over to me and say, "Violette can I disturb you?" And then he would say what he wanted to tell you but he would always first say, "May I disturb you?" It was mostly in class and we would know that it might have to do with our habits. He had better habits for us and he was hoping we would change.

It's a given that not all students will go on to dance careers. Verdy spoke to these realities:

> You can adore ballet and be built all wrong. Adoring ballet doesn't make you right for the part, so to speak. Just because you happen to be attracted to a particular art form, it doesn't grant you the right of passage. But if you have it in your heart, and you continue, there must be talent there somewhere, and sometimes later on you find yourself doing things that at a younger age you thought were incomprehensible.

To Verdy, talent is a God-given gift that a person carries with him or her through life. "It doesn't stop as you get older," she said. "Perhaps it even grows in a certain direction, branching off from its initial cocoon. Sometimes our dancers decide they don't want to do it professionally and then turn to other forms of dance and it turns out well." Or talent can go in a different direction entirely. IU offers those students who will not make it into the professional ranks many alternatives, including medicine, journalism and law. Verdy explained the transition process:

> Ballet dancers are usually very intelligent. They tend to want to be in control of things. Many of our students who decide not to continue can't wait to get out to do other things and rise to heights in other fields. You want to give them time to take responsibility, to emotionally recognize the place they are in. You wait until they already know. But you continually stress, "Find out what you're good at—you should pursue that."

Verdy believes the process can be eased and lightened by the teacher, so that students lose less time and suffer less. She chuckled, "We are really only the midwives—we deliver the baby."

In October 2010, Indiana University Jacobs School of Music announced they had received the gift of an endowment to support the first faculty chair in classical ballet in the nation. Distinguished Professor Violette Verdy was the inaugural recipient of the Kathy Ziliak Anderson Chair Award.

This career culmination was followed by a discouraging and exhausting year in 2011 as Verdy was diagnosed with a herniated disc. She alternated visits to doctors with her teaching responsibilities at IU. Surgery was an option, but she refused. "Of course the whole idea is to go on. You know dancers are a lot braver than they are patient," she said. Ultimately her condition necessitated her taking time off. But Verdy drew from prior experience. She had endured several injuries during her career, dating back to the days with Roland Petit, including tendonitis in her ankles.

At one point she had stopped dancing cold turkey, then realized that was not the best thing to have done. As a dancer she realized how important it was for her to continue to take care of herself, so she started going to the gym regularly and doing a lot of barre to get back in shape. That same approach saw her through the recovery process from the herniated disc in later life.

Perseverance ultimately paid off and in 2015, 70 years into her professional career, Verdy was invited to be guest teacher in the summer program at the Paris Opera Ballet. Along with her teaching and directing responsibilities, Verdy has continued to serve on many boards over the years. When asked how she managed to do it all, she simply said, "I did it."

Juliet Seignious

From Bourbon to Ballet

"I started ballet lessons because I couldn't spell." Juliet Seignious' mother had told her father that their daughter was having trouble reading in school, so he brought out his bourbon bottle to test her. "I pronounced it phonetically, 'bauer a ban,'" she remembered. "He thought I was dyslexic—he was so distressed, he said, 'I think I should put you in dancing school,' because he thought that I wasn't going to be a scholar. "Maybe you can be another Lena Horne," she remembered him saying. "It turned out to be the most wonderful decision," she said, "and that was the beginning."

Seignious started ballet and tap at Mary Bruce's little studio on 125th St. and Morningside Avenue in Harlem. For Seignious, it was love at first sight. "I didn't know anything about ballet until I went to this school," said Seignious. "Not only was Mary a wonderful teacher, she taught you how to listen to music and let the music move you."

At age four, she gave her first dance recital at Carnegie Hall. She had two solos: one ballet, and one tap in which she also sang. Her family could only afford two costumes so her tap costume also served for the group number. "It came to eight dollars—today it would cost about $200 for a ballet costume and that's the cheapest," she said. It was the first time her father had ever seen her dance. She remembered how proud he was:

> He loved it—he was very surprised. He was a musician, tending to his plumbing contracting during the day and playing the trumpet and guitar at night. He would sit around the wood-burning stove in his plumbing shop and tell his buddies that his daughter was a ballet dancer. He was very proud because he was the one who started me on the venture.

Her mother was not as emotionally or artistically invested in her dancing, but went along with it. "I think it was because of her background," said Seignious. "She was from Charleston, S.C., and never got above fifth grade. She worked as a domestic. Her dimensions of knowledge were not as great as my father's." Seignious described her mother as being equally supportive, but in a different direction:

> She always washed my leotard and tights. That was very important because we couldn't afford a lot of them so she would make sure that my bag was always packed and everything was clean and my hair was always combed a certain way. It was how she identified with what I was doing.

Seignious had five brothers and six sisters. With the exception of one brother, all were from previous marriages on both sides. Seignious was the youngest. No one else in the family danced, but they were proud of her. "You'd think it was my sister who danced," said Seignious, "because she'd take me to dancing school then come home and tell everybody everything I did."

In junior high school Seignious discovered an after-school ballet club and became more and more deeply involved in ballet. Her teacher, Ms. Roberts, arranged for eight of the girls to audition for Performing Arts High School. She recalled the pointe class for the audition, in which the teacher demonstrated everything with her hands. "Coming from my background, I wondered what in the world she was doing," she recalled. "I had to watch the other students to know what was going on." Seignious was the only one accepted from her school, joining a class that included Eliot Feld and Louis Falco.

"I was thrilled and scared," she recalled. "I had come from a school in Harlem where there were no white students. It was a big adjustment for me." In addition, her fellow students had been taking lessons since they were three or four years old. She realized she had a lot of catching up to do technically. But since the school had accepted her, she figured there had to be something about her that they were impressed with.

After a year at PA she was told by the head of the dance department that while she was a very good dancer, she would have better opportunities in the dance world if she switched from ballet to modern. "She said because I was 'colored' I was going to have a very difficult time…at that time, they said 'colored.'" Seignious went home and told her mother, who said, "Well maybe that's best, if she feels you can get a job as a dancer."

In her junior year, at age 18, Seignious performed in a PA dance concert at Hunter College. The concert was attended by faculty at the School of American Ballet, who after seeing her solo, went to the PA department head and told her to put Seignious back in the ballet track, at the same time expressing interest in her future career. Seignious recalls the impact that had on her:

> I just couldn't believe it. The first thought that popped into my head was, "Okay, you told me there would be no

blacks in a ballet company and nobody would be interested in me," and here the School of American Ballet was offering me a scholarship.

New York City Ballet had one black artist at the time, Arthur Mitchell, whose talent was such that he had crossed the color line. Seignious was to learn that NYCB wanted Mitchell to have a black partner. "Not exactly integration," she said, wryly. Seignious had never met Mitchell, but he soon got in touch. "Arthur told me this would be my greatest opportunity," she said.

Seignious started at SAB, studying with Muriel Stuart, whom she described as her "jumping teacher":

> I was a jumper and she always had me jumping with the boys. I had to work harder than anybody else, especially en pointe because I had not had a lot of pointe work. But at the School of American Ballet, I really got it. I realized how lucky I was.

She recalls being asked to sign a paper stipulating she would not get married. While Balanchine never communicated with her directly, she suspects he was behind it (she married anyway, at 20, keeping it a secret). She remembers him watching class from the top of the stairs, leaning on the railing which surrounded the studio, and thinking to herself, "Pull up. Stay en pointe. Do your pirouettes and don't fall." She recalls Balanchine never watched the barre, just the floor work. "He wanted to see us dance!" she said. While Balanchine wanted his dancers to be tall, slender and long-limbed, Seignious was comparatively short, but it didn't seem to make any difference—she was sought after.

Mitchell had warned her about the problems she might run into with other female dancers, telling her it wasn't going to be easy. "I think he was talking about color. Word got around that I was a special student, with the potential of joining the company so there was a lot of jealousy."

At about the same time that NYCB was pursuing Seignious, Alvin Ailey was looking for ballet dancers for his company. When he heard she was at SAB with a company apprenticeship, he immediately offered her a job. She knew that staying with NYCB would secure her future, while Ailey had no name or reputation yet. But he was persistent, and had an advantage:¶

> Alvin was doing dances that were dealing with my heritage. I remember thinking that at NYCB I was going to be doing white ballet that would not really relate to me. I asked myself, "Do I go with Alvin who doesn't have a name or do I stay at NYCB, an established company with a secure future?" At Ailey we were talking rehearsals at the YMCA on 8th Avenue.

In the midst of this difficult decision, Seignious recalls taking a class at SAB with Madame Doubrovska:

> We had to do 64 échappées en pointe. By the time I got to 42, I thought "Is she serious?" My toes started bleeding through the pink shoes. I remember going to the locker room and sitting there, staring at my bloody feet, all the while thinking, "Do I really want to go through this?" I thought, "Arthur will be mad at me. This is such a good opportunity," but I really wanted to know more about my heritage.

She decided to go with Ailey, becoming one of that company's founding members in 1958. She recalled feeling sad about leaving NYCB, but figured eventually she would be happier being around people who understood her. At NYCB the only friend she had was Mitchell, and recalls thinking that for him it was different: "Arthur's parents came from the West Indies. People from the West Indies had a whole different mindset than African-Americans who came here through slavery."

While Ailey was the best option for a black ballet dancer at the time, Seignious said Bernard Johnson was also looking to start an all-black ballet company at that time in New York City. Like Seignious, he was feeling the isolation of being an African-American ballet dancer in an exclusively white profession: "He felt, since no one was going to have us as ballet dancers, why not start our own company?" Seignious recalls there were three women interested in the venture: Cleo Quitman, Yvonne McDowell, and herself, and on the men's side Johnson, Dudley Williams, and one other. The group tried unsuccessfully to get state and federal funding. "At the time, Albany was donating money for dance companies to visit other countries in order to promote the arts," Seignious recalled. "But it was too early for funding a black dance company." The racism in ballet hit McDowell particularly hard:

> She was a black female dancer who had also attended PA She was so in love with ballet—she was crazed for it. She ended up committing suicide because no ballet company would accept her because of her color. And here I was. I had the opportunity that Yvonne would have loved to have had and yet I left NYCB to go to Alvin.

By 1963, the Ailey Company was funded to visit Japan with the stated purpose of bringing people together. It was the first black company ever to visit and perform abroad. Seignious also helped pave the way for blacks on television, appearing on the Gary Moore Show in the '60s. "It was the first time they hired a black man and woman to be on TV. Before that there was Mercedes Ellington, who was a June Taylor dancer, but she was fair-skinned so she fit in with the line of girls and nobody could tell the difference," said Seignious.

After many years with Ailey, Seignious joined up with Donald McKayle, the first African-American man to choreograph and direct major Broadway musicals. Seiginois was able to bring her two-year-old son, Chris, with her when she taught and danced for McKayle in Europe. Although the pay was only $60 a week, she was delighted. Initially she felt very apprehensive about dancing in Germany, having been told that the Germans hated black people, but she found them extremely friendly and generous, especially to her son. From this she learned an important lesson herself about prejudging others:

> I remember passengers on a bus gave me a down blanket for my son, to make sure he stayed warm. I hired a German babysitter and she just loved him. I made two resolutions: Don't let other people tell you what to think or what other people are like.

Eventually Seignious began to limit her performing and increase her teaching in order to spend more time with her son. But she missed the special connection she had with the audience whenever she performed. With Ailey especially, she felt the audience always understood what they were trying to do. "They connected with the dancers. It was always joyous to see the audience getting up and clapping. It was the same with Donny McKayle." She doesn't believe she would have ever experienced that same feeling had she remained with NYCB.

Seignious has been through numerous career transitions: from ballerina to modern dancer, to choreographer, to teacher, to painter, but through it all, she continues to think of herself primarily as a dancer. "It's because of what dance has given me over all these years," she said. "Ballet brought me out of Harlem. It took me from a minimal way of living and brought me to a larger scope," she said.

While her teaching of late has centered on modern dance, she is convinced that ballet training makes for a better modern dancer:

> Ballet gives you the line that is so beautiful regardless of what kind of dancing you are doing. Balanchine was aware of that. Along with the line comes artistry. It is not an easy thing to teach. But the sooner they can begin to learn it, the better.

Beyond technique, Seignious focuses on making the movement meaningful to her students: "I am constantly drumming it into them—dance with your heart." She finds the work ethic of many of today's students lacking:

> Students today are very different from forty or fifty years ago. Back then, dance was a privilege. You didn't take it for granted when you were in class. Today, kids think it's something that belongs to them and therefore working hard does not mean the same thing as it did then. They are not used to pain. When you give a combination, they'll come in the next day complaining about how sore they are. I will always say that's part of dancing. You get

sore because you are retraining your muscles. Both ballet and modern dance require a great deal of strength—without it, you are a candidate for injury.

At 75, Seignious attributed her youthful appearance and outlook to dance. "Dance is such a positive thing," she said. "Stress is really the number one killer. I think from stress all kinds of things happen. Having danced, and still dancing when I teach, keeps the mind peaceful," she said. When aches and pains come she sits herself down and says, "All right now, let's do this." The dancer in her knows she can push through. "It's like Tai Chi. Energy flows through my body, and then I get up and move on."

Robert Maiorano

From Hell to Heaven

As a ballet student growing up in a Brooklyn neighborhood between Bedford-Stuyvesant and Williamsburg, Robert Maiorano was called names every day of his life. "Half of the boys in my neighborhood didn't know what ballet was, the other half made fun of me."

Maiorano lost his father before he was two. His mother told him stories about how his father, an amateur boxer who had fought at St. Nick's Arena in New York City, learned how to avoid fights. Because his dad had won 54 bouts, losing only two, and had never been knocked off his feet, this was taken as a challenge by neighborhood toughs.

> People knew he was a boxer, and they would say after a couple of drinks, 'Okay, let's see how tough you are.' But because he was a trained boxer, if my father had hit somebody he could have been sued, so he learned how to talk his way out of a fight. I remember my mother continually saying, 'It is a stronger thing to be able to talk your way out of a fight then to fight.' So my father, indirectly, gave me the power to talk my way out of a fight. That's how I got out of my neighborhood in one piece.

Maiorano remembers using his ballet training to his advantage in encounters with neighborhood kids:

> By 11, I had learned how to do a double tour and I showed them. A couple of times, the leader would say, 'That's nothing,' and jump up and try to turn twice in the air, but land on his head instead of his feet. My friends would all be laughing, but I helped him up and gained respect.

Maiorano was born in August of 1946, and started dancing "officially" at age eight. He recalled, "I actually started at age three, just for a couple of months, at a local school. They took everybody's money, and then skipped town—it was a franchise of Fred Astaire Dance Studios." After studying ballet for six months he made his TV debut on *The Merry Mailman* TV show around 1950:

> I didn't know what was happening on the show—I was three years old, and never had a TV. This girl and I held hands above our heads, and looked at each other. Bing Crosby's voice was in the background, singing the hit song of the season, *White Christmas*. We were on the 82nd floor of the Empire State Building. The best thing about it was looking out of the window.

Maiorano continued his ballet lessons, inspired by the first ballet he ever saw: Ballet Theatre's *Billy the Kid* with John Kriza. "I knew the story. I remember that dark stage with the spotlight just following Billy around. It was mesmerizing," he said. Soon he was offered a scholarship to the School of American Ballet. He recalled his years in the building housed on 59th St. off Madison Avenue and later at the great space at 82nd St. and Broadway:

There were all those wonderful teachers: Antonina Tumkovsky, who had escaped from the Ukraine when the Nazis invaded in 1938; former Mariinsky stars Anatole Oboukhoff and Pierre Vladimirov; Muriel Stuart, who had danced with Pavlova; former Ballets Russes ballerina Felia Doubrovska; and Hélène Dudin, who migrated to the United States from Europe after World War II. She gave me a family size Hershey's chocolate bar as a present after my first year.

In his second year at the school Maiorano was given his first taste of the stage. "Wow! This is great! I'm backstage," he remembers thinking, as he stood in the wings at New York City Center in his soldier's costume, waiting to perform in *The Nutcracker*. It was the 1950s and he was the only boy in his class. Sixteen soldiers danced in that production: 15 girls and Robert Maiorano. He remembers being fascinated by the ropes and the pulleys and watching the dancers put on their makeup. "The costume didn't mean much to me. It was the atmosphere, being backstage and suddenly you step out two feet and you're on stage. That was the big deal."

In subsequent *Nutcracker* seasons Maiorano performed as Fritz (the brother of Clara) before dancing the Prince for three years. He recalled the TV special of *Nutcracker*, directed by Balanchine, who was also playing Drossselmeyer:

> We were waiting, off camera, to go on—our first entrance was together. Balanchine was standing next to me and he kept asking, 'Do we go now?' He started to go on, and I said, 'No, no,' and I had to keep holding him back. Then, I said, 'OK, now!' I was 12 years old, and I remember wondering why Balanchine didn't know when to go on. I didn't know at the time how much he had on his mind.

André Eglevsky had had a heart attack, and Balanchine had to rechoreograph the famous pas de deux using the four *divertissement* soloists. Our entrance was the last thing he was thinking about.

Maiorano's idol in the company was Eglevsky. "When I was a little boy, Eglevsky was the leading dancer of New York City Ballet and the great dancer of his day, along with Igor Youskevitch over at Ballet Theatre. Eglevsky was always very nice to me; he was like a father." At one point Eglevsky gave Maiorano a boy scout knife, and used to invite him to come into his dressing room to watch him put on his makeup.

Maiorano has vivid memories of the day at the School of American Ballet, while taking Anatole Oboukhoff's class, when things suddenly came together:

> I was doing a diagonal combination across the floor. I remember the feeling of the air as I went flying across the room and thinking "I'm free, I'm flying! Power! Strength! I'm higher than anyone else I ever saw in this room!" That was the moment that I knew I wanted to become a dancer.

At 15 he was asked to join the company, beginning a 22-year career. His favorite soloist roles were in the Frederick Ashton ballet *Illuminations*, and *Dances at a Gathering*, which he referred to as Jerome Robbins' masterpiece.

His only hiatus from the company came after he injured his knee. He remembered, "I wasn't dancing for six months so I started writing. At first I wrote for catharsis, to be able to deal with the injury." He had never written as a youngster, but had always done well in English Composition in school, despite not particularly enjoying the class, or school in general: "Given the choice, I'd always have rather been playing baseball," he said. But an early love interest turned his intellectual life around:

> When I was 19, I had a girlfriend who was a dancer at NYCB. She left her diary open one night, and I looked at it. It was early in the relationship. She had written about me: "A body like a Greek god, but where are the brains?" I wasn't stupid, but I had never graduated high school. The next day, we went to the bookstore. I got Camus, Kafka, de Beauvoir, Sartre and Baudelaire. And, after that, I never stopped reading.

Maiorano retired from NYCB in 1983, the same year Balanchine died. As one of the company's most popular soloists, he hadn't planned for a time when he would no longer perform. "Toward the end, I thought I'd just write and live on the beach by the ocean," he said.

He was 37 when he transitioned to an acting career, at first joining a mime company for two years. He recalled, "They had an audition, I went, they looked at my resume, and even though I had had no mime experience, they figured since I had been a dancer with NYCB I could learn easily." He performed in a mime version of Dracula at Town Hall, and taught a few days a week for income. The rest of the time he freelanced, took acting classes, and went out on auditions.

The writing spark, lit during a period of injury, kept burning. Maiorano has written several books, including his autobiography, the synopsis of Balanchine's The *Nutcracker* that appears in the NYCB program each year, and a book about the creation of Balanchine's ballet *Mozartiana*, which he wrote while still a dancer with NYCB. The book follows the process of the ballet's creation, from the first rehearsal to opening night. Maiorano explained his own process:

> I wasn't dancing much in those days. Balanchine let me remain in the studio during the rehearsals. He wanted to use Ib Andersen and Suzanne Farrell. I sat next to the piano, or under it, for hours. I decided not to take notes because it would be a distraction so I'd just sit there concentrating and then run to my dressing room and write down everything I could remember. Then, after my performance, I'd go home and transfer it to a first draft.

Currently, Maiorano is on the faculty of the Glens Falls Ballet and Dance Center in Queensbury, N.Y. He is a resident of Saratoga Springs, and co-founded the Saratoga City Ballet School in the 1980s, with Patti Pugh Henderer, a dancer from the North Carolina School of the Arts. It was subsequently sold to two Skidmore graduates.

What does he look for in a student? "There are a lot of things to look for," he said, "the proportions of the body, long-limbed, long neck, decent feet, strength, passion, and determination. Some kids are more determined than others." He continued, "musicality, focus, work-ethic, technical proficiency, and you need talent. You either have it or you don't. That's what wins out ultimately." But even with talent, his best advice to students is that "you have to work like hell to dance like heaven."

Maiorano's thoughts on artistry are understandably shaped by Balanchine, who believed an artist uses all five senses. "Balanchine said what made him an artist was that he could see and hear better than anyone else." Such sensitivity can prolong a career in dance:

> Even if you can no longer do a step, you can continue to work, with artistry, to get a feeling in the arch of the neck or in your eyes. The choices that you make in performance are the mark of an artist, and it comes with experience.

Maiorano reflected on life after dance. "Of course ageing changes the body. I didn't get fat, but I'm not lean anymore. My weakness is sweets. I never took drugs or indulged in alcohol." There are also the changes to one's self-image, or self-definition:

> Even though I'm referred to as a dancer every day by everybody else, I no longer think of myself as one. Today, I make other people dance, and I'm a choreographer. I call myself a teacher. It's nice to be remembered, but life goes on. But after you stop dancing, you still want the respect from your peers. I'm still in touch with Jacques d'Amboise and Frank Ohman.

He also still exercises. "Not enough," he said grinning, adding, "I do practice the Five Tibetan Rites." He described it as a sort of yoga for the endocrine glands. He has also devised his own series of exercises, "Pilates with weights," and walks everywhere. He can still do an entrechat six.

He enjoys coaching professional dancers, and said he can coach anything at NYCB. "We always taught our part to someone else in NYCB. Professional dancers put themselves in your hands as a coach, we point out something that they weren't aware of, or how to get the momentum going, or how to do a step."

He would like to see more dance instruction in the New York State public schools. "All public schools have volleyball and baseball teams, but how many have dance instruction? It's all so different today…" he paused and added, "and nobody is playing hopscotch in the street anymore." To illustrate his point, Maiorano related a humorous incident while choreographing a piece for the Saratoga City Ballet:

> I was told to use as many students as possible. I told this 10 year-old girl to make her entrance, skipping, and she didn't know what I was talking about. She had never skipped. I had to stop everything, and teach her to skip. What is the world coming to when a 50 year-old man has to teach a 10 year-old girl how to skip?

Carol Bryan

A Pivot From Dance

"Fulfilling, adventurous, and educational." That's how Carol Bryan, Director of Education for the Palace Theater in Stamford, Connecticut, summed up her careers. Bryan stands as an example to dancers whose performance careers are cut short by injury.

Bryan's tale is typical of the professional dancer: full of early promise, fueled by an inner passion for dance. "It all started at age six," she said. "I was very shy. I never danced around the house, but I always looked forward to my dance classes. I felt it was something that was mine. It was my own world, where I could express myself. There was something very calming about it."

She felt different in elementary school. "Of all the kids, I was the only one dancing. It was a serious work environment at the School of American Ballet from the time I was eight." She remembered the audition to get into the School of American Ballet. "I auditioned before Hélène Dudin and Antonina Tumkovsky. Dudin was very soft spoken and very kind. I wasn't afraid of her at the audition, but I was afraid of Tumkovsky. She seemed much more demanding and louder.

Bryan studied with Tumkovsky for eight years, along with Dudin, and all the Russian faculty, including Felia Doubrovska and Alexandra Danilova. She remembered Doubrovska, who was married to Pierre Vladimirov, used to come to the school with two little Yorkies. "They were not in the studio. They stayed in the dressing room." When she got older, she also studied with Muriel Stuart and Stanley Williams. At 16, she lost the drive for ballet:

> I remember just wanting to be a regular kid and hang out after school with my friends. I gave away all my pointe shoes and ballet slippers. I was living in two different worlds and I had to find out which world I belonged in.

When she told her parents, it was fine with them. After three weeks of not showing up for class, the school called. Her mother told them Carol didn't want to be there anymore.

The hiatus turned out to be short-lived, but crucial. "I knew I wanted something more for my life, but it was so boring," she said. "I experienced that other life for three weeks, and there was nothing special about it at all." Suddenly she knew ballet was something she had to do. She returned to SAB and her ballet friends.

Bryan remained at SAB until she was almost 17, when she was told she was too small for the company. Her mother took her out of SAB and enrolled her in The Joffrey Ballet School, where she studied for a year. Patricia Wilde, then a ballet mistress at American Ballet Theatre, taught there and one day invited Bryan to a closed audition for ABT. The audition included eighty candidates and lasted four days, but at the end of the fourth day she was offered a contract.

Bryan danced with ABT for four and a half years until she developed a severe case of bursitis in her hip. She was barely 23. After taking a great deal of time off she auditioned for two other companies: the Pennsylvania Ballet, and Agnes De Mille Dance Theatre, and guested around the country as the Sugar Plum Fairy in *The Nutcracker*, but her hip problems persisted. She became nervous on stage because she wasn't performing enough. She started spending more of her time teaching, Bryan doesn't recall when she decided to stop dancing entirely. "It just sort of evolved," she said.

The years went by. Bryan raised a family while teaching part-time, but preferred spending most of her time at home with her children. The only time she really missed performing was when she went to performances, especially ABT, and especially ballets in which she had danced. "I would sit in my seat in the theater and do all the choreography in my head and my legs and my feet would move," she recalled.

Looking to do something beyond teaching, Bryan went to Career Transitions for Dancers, a program designed to help dancers turn the discipline, skills and focus learned in the studio into other careers. She was awarded a scholarship for computer training, and ultimately discovered a passion and talent for arts administration.

As Director of Education for the Palace Theatre in Stamford, Bryan creates and implements programs in the performing arts for children and young adults. "I feel like I'm changing one life at a time," she said. "Each child has different abilities, passions, and desires, and I can help nurture them through the teachers that I work with." The programs she has created include a young choreographer's festival and a playwriting festival. Her fundraising efforts with sponsors, donors, and grant programs allow her to do all that she wants to do from year to year.

Bryan remembers being a young dancer set on the idea that she only wanted to dance with a New York company, when her mother gave her some good advice: "If you love to dance, you can dance anywhere." Bryan now passes that advice along to her students, and broadens it beyond performing:

> Dance because you love to dance, but don't limit yourself. Try new things. Nowadays, there are so many opportunities to be creative with a dance background, to have careers in dance that are non-performing. When you're a performer, it's all about you. Now, it's about giving my vision and my voice to these children.

Marilyn K. Miller
Overcoming the Odds

"Fifty thousand back port de bras, 25,000 grand jetés, 100,000 jetés and assemblés and pirouettes, and pointe shoes that didn't fit, floors that weren't sprung…" says Marilyn Miller, Studio Owner of Pilates on Hudson, listing causes of her many injuries which saddled her ballet career early on. There were mornings in such pain that her first few attempts to get out of bed sent her right back to bed again. But there were enough successes to keep her going, like receiving one of the few full scholarships to the University of Utah's Dance Department.

Bryan's tale is typical of the professional dancer: full of early promise, fueled by an inner passion for dance. "It all started at age six," she said. "I was very shy. I never danced around the house, but I always looked forward to my dance classes. I felt it was something that was mine. It was my own world, where I could express myself. There was something very calming about it."

She remembers being four, going to the Piggly Wiggly grocery store in Dallas, Texas with her mother and seeing the little dance school next door:

> I remember seeing the little girls in their pink tights and black leotards, and I have no idea why, because nobody in my family danced, but I tugged on my mother's shorts

and started shouting, "Mommy, Mommy, I want to dance! I want to dance!" I had never seen a ballet. I had no idea what a ballerina was. I just knew I wanted to be one.

She began lessons at the Dallas Metropolitan School of Ballet with Ann Etkin and Phil Atkinson, with whom she studied for about ten years before joining their semi-professional company at age 13. Miller says her parents were Depression babies, "but they wanted to provide my brothers and me with all the opportunities they didn't have growing up in a small rural town." They paid for all her dance lessons and supported their children "regardless of how they felt about our ability to earn a living," she said. She made the decision to pursue a professional dance career before college, while her older brother became a musician/sound engineer with The Nitty Gritty Dirt Band and her younger brother became a theatrical lighting designer.

As a teenager she danced with the Dallas Opera, before leaving for Salt Lake City and the scholarship at the University of Utah. After two years, students were given the chance to work with Ballet West, but while Miller got picked to perform with the company and was even given a soloist role, at season's end she wasn't offered a contract. Instead, she recalled the director, John Hart, suggesting that she "go to Las Vegas." Miller says she had always been cast as the gypsy or the floozy, and yet the director "was not comfortable with my sensuality—I don't think I ultimately played into his very British idea of what a ballerina should look like."

Instead of staying on at the University of Utah, Miller joined the Eugene Ballet in Eugene, Oregon, a small company with only sixteen dancers. "I was one of two principal female dancers, there were two principal male dancers, and the rest made up the soloists and corps de ballet." Life at this level of the dance world was not easy. "There was no money in the budget for shoes, so we always danced in shoes that were past their prime," she said. There were no sprung floors either. "I blew out my ankles on a stage designed to hold a full-blown orchestra," she said, "and there was little time for rehab. I remember coming home at the end of the day and literally putting both of my ankles on ice."

After dancing with the Eugene Ballet for a year, Miller auditioned for and contracted to dance with San Francisco Opera Ballet, but they only did short-term contracts and the season was rarely more than 15 weeks. In between seasons, she picked up whatever kind of work she could. She guested with local companies, including Santa Clara Ballet (performing the Lilac Fairy in *The Sleeping Beauty*) and Peninsula Ballet Theatre (performing Myrtha in *Giselle*). She worked with Alonzo King, Founder and Artistic Director of Alonzo King LINES Ballet, and got her start doing choreography as performer/choreographer with the Underworld Opera Company, now Oakland Opera Theater, where she worked on-and-off for many years and learned how to run a small not-for-profit arts organization.

Miller said her story is not a glamorous one, but a much more common one in terms of how most people's dance careers really go:

> They don't usually play out like I've got a contract with SFB, and I'm there for ten years, and then I go to Boston, and I'm there for ten years. They do play out like I'm doing a lot of different things all at the same time. I was always doing something, but there wasn't much money, and I doubt anyone had insurance.

She primarily supported herself by working as a legal secretary by day, and dancing nights and weekends. She did pet sitting. Sometimes, if she did have insurance, she was able to get treatment for previous injuries. Ultimately, she received a "lifetime settlement" from worker's compensation insurance for the ankle injury suffered at the State Ballet of Oregon, a total of $5,000. "Yep, some lifetime," she said. Reflecting on that period in her career she added somberly, "It was kind of sad, really."

Ultimately, a fellow dancer suggested that she visit the Center for Dance Medicine at St. Francis Hospital, to get proper attention for her injuries:

> I don't know if it changed my life, but it certainly put me on a path toward where I was going. They had an entire program in which the orthopedists saw the dancers, made a diagnosis, and then the dancers went into physical therapy. Pilates was a component of the post-rehabilitation phase of any kind of an injury. It was the Ritz-Carlton of physical therapy. They had me doing things on the Pilates equipment and I got better. In fact, I got so much better, I was better than before I got injured. And I thought, maybe I can do this for a second career when I grow up.

She found a Martha Graham dance studio. "I looked in, and saw that for at least 45 minutes of the class, I could be sitting on the floor," she said. This held appeal as she continued to rehab her ankles:

> I could do Graham breathing contractions. It was wonderful to be able to express myself. But it was the amount of work we had to do with our feet, working through the flexed foot, that helped the ankles to slowly start to get better.

When the feet got better, she was able to go back to King and continue with ballet. "Then I completely blew out my back," she said. She had degenerative disc disease, rotator cuff issues and knee issues. She became depressed, and remembers bursting into tears, asking herself, "What do I do now?"

She relocated to New York. An orthopedist at a local dance center went over her X-rays and diagnosis, walked into the exam room, and told her that her back wasn't ever going to get better. "He was basically confirming the end of my career in less than five minutes."

Miller applied for and got a job at the Martha Graham Dance Company as company manager for the senior company. She went to a gym, tried aerobics, but it was too painful. There was another round of doctor's visits. She did Pilates again, which took her out of her permanent pain, instilling in her a deep understanding of the anatomy of the body. She enrolled in a training program to become a Pilates personal trainer, received her certification but after a few years realized it was not enough:

> I kept telling people what to do and showing them how to do it, but at some point I realized what really needed to happen was to teach the clients the way I was taught as a dancer: piece by piece and step by step, with a clear understanding of what the movement was, where it was coming from, and what the end goal was.

This is now her mission at Pilates on Hudson. "Every day I do some kind of Pilates. I keep in shape because I teach a class that I participate in," she said. A typical week has her in the studio for ten hours a day, Monday through Friday, and Saturday mornings.

Miller starts at a very basic level, teaching about the different planes of motion in the body:

> Nobody understands what they are and why we need to limit our movements within these planes of motion. This is all the stuff I learned as a ballet dancer. Because it is physiologically correct, it means I am less likely to get injured as I get older. Most people have to start with the very basics, like a child. You have to know how to stand and where you place your feet. Usually the best students are people who have a history of rehabilitation that has not been productive, so they are happy to finally have someone sit down and explain to them what is going on.

Miller has also started practicing yoga, and sees a connection between yoga and dance. "Yoga influenced Pilates when he was developing his technique," she said. "Graham, too, was influenced by yoga. One begets the other. You think about the arabesque in ballet, it's related to the warrior position in yoga."

Now when Miller looks back at her career in ballet she thinks, "It was a very narcissistic thing to do." She remembers times in her career when she asked herself, "Why am I doing this?' All I am doing is twirling around on stage. There's got to be more to life." She believes she has found that: "What I am doing now is giving back to people what I have learned, and I am giving something back to the community."

Recently she has been seeing a lot more dance, and is beginning to make her peace. "I have always had a belief in dance as the truest form of expression," she said. Today when she dances, she does it simply because she wants to dance:

> I don't care if I'm broken, or if my leg doesn't go up very high. Even if I can't do classical ballet anymore, I still have something to say. When I first started dancing, when I was a kid, I wanted to dance because I loved to dance. And then I started seeing I was good at it, and I wanted to be better than the other dancers, and I wanted to work with a bigger company, and I wanted a better job, and I wanted to make more money and it got to a point where it was more about the external accomplishments as opposed to the internal. You start out loving ballet and dancing, and the more you go into it, the more perfect you have to be—you have to kick higher, jump further, turn more, but it gets to a point where it's like you're trying to split the atom and that perfectionism turns really negative because there is no such thing as perfect. I think a post-dance career is finding a way out of that. I'm still finding it, but with a confidence I have never had before.

Karole Armitage
Exploring Life's Mysteries

Karole Armitage speaks in an explosion of energy—you can barely keep up with her. Choreographer, dancer, teacher, artistic ballet director, innovator—for Armitage, ballet is far more than a series of steps or set of rules. In fact, her choreography doesn't look like ballet at all. She describes it as "a conceptual tool for moving on and off balance." Far from making things simpler, her approach complicates: "It is much harder to be innovative in this way of thinking," she explained.

But that has always been Armitage's way—to not repeat the usual ways of doing things. "The way ballet is organized traditionally is very much about horizontal and vertical lines," she said. "But there is something about timbre," (which she defined as the weight of a sound that corresponds to a feeling of weight in the body) "the rhythmic drive of those timbres has a design to it that suggest special movement." She said her choreography is based on fractal geometry, which she describes as, "the geometry of the natural world", for example, mountains and clouds. But far as she may branch, her roots are in ballet.

Armitage's life in dance started in Lawrence, Kansas at age six. Tomi Wortham, a former member of New York City Ballet, came to Lawrence and Armitage started ballet lessons three times a week.

She was introduced to Balanchine's choreography and after learning *Serenade* and *Gounod Symphony* for the season recital she was hooked.

When Wortham left town, Armitage discovered Tatiana Dokoudovska in Kansas City, where her mother drove her for lessons, one hour each way, for several years. At age 13, she went to New York City for the summer to study at the School of American Ballet and the Harkness Ballet School. Armitage did not want to leave when the season was over, but her parents were not about to let their daughter remain in New York for the winter. She returned to Lawrence where she studied in several schools closer to home, as well as the North Carolina School of the Arts, where she went at age 15.

Her first professional job was with Ballet du Grand Théâtre de Genève in the mid 70's, where Balanchine was the artistic advisor. Armitage studied with him, along with several other NYCB dancers. Anxious to explore new ideas, she returned to New York where she began classes with Merce Cunningham. After six months, she was invited to join his company. She credits Cunningham with being a tremendous influence and inspiration on her work:

> It was fascinating to learn a new way to move, but I wasn't going to throw away all those years of ballet. Cunningham did make use of a great deal of ballet technique while he invented this new way of using space and a new way of using music. He is responsible for changing the conception of dance. He broke down the hierarchy of how we see dance. His influence is now in every choreographer's tool box. Take Alexei Ratmansky—we see the Cunningham influence there. He has people facing the back of the stage, and no one person is more important than the other. Space is a field where everyone is equally important and two or more activities can be seen at the same time. This is the opposite of framing the important person all the time, for example, the corps framing the prima ballerina in the royal tradition.

Armitage stopped performing in 1989, at age 34. She views her transition to choreographer and artistic director as an outgrowth of her performing career:

> While I was dancing I was also running my company, Armitage Gone! Dance, as well as choreographing and doing administration fundraising. I felt while I was dancing, I couldn't contribute fully to all of these things, so I wasn't doing any of them to the highest level that I aspired to. I had danced so much—there was nothing left unfinished, and it was wonderful to be a choreographer because it was asking more of my mind.

Armitage has explored working without music in her choreographic work:

> Surprisingly, some of the purest classical dancers are the best at it. They are so deeply attuned to their bodies that dancing to the body's rhythm and sense of time is natural. For example, in 1983, I worked with Sylvie Guillem and Isabelle Guérin of Paris Opera Ballet. They were very comfortable moving without music and understood how body language moving in time is deeply expressive with no need of further support to convey meaning. Dancers are remarkably precise. The sense of the physical rhythm in a good dancer is so great that a group of dancers can rehearse or perform an hour-long dance without sound and it will not vary in time more than two seconds. You listen to each other much as a flock of birds flies together. The listening is very powerful and creates a marvelous, mysterious concentration

that is compelling to watch and experience from the audience. For over 60 years, the most innovative work in dance has been done without dancing directly to music. The focus of attention is on the body language, which has its own deep musicality and expressivity. But I do not think the lack of structured music—a musical phrase that carries the body along—is necessarily tied to a compromise in innovation.

The thirst for discovery through innovation is at the heart of Armitage's philosophy:

Like all innovation, one needs to think in new ways. In the great ballets, the story is only a pretext for great dancing that reveals the mysterious, irrational parts of our existence. Theater is good at that. With theater, you understand complex social relationships, but dance cannot do that because there are no words. But what you can see in dance is the inner life of people through the expression of their body language. It is a time for recognizing themselves in what they see so they can think about their lives—a time for contemplation. I'm trying to explore life's mysteries and my own connection to these moments. There is nothing as satisfying as dancing because you use every part of what it is to be human: your intelligence, emotion, psychology, eroticism, your entire physical body at the very same moment.

Armitage describes the work of a choreographer as "a lonely venture." She feels that choreographers, more than dancers, are prey to criticism and misunderstanding: "For an audience, it is easier to love and appreciate the wonderful dancer, but the choreographer's presence is more elusive and more controversial because it is more complicated to understand what the choreographer is doing, as opposed to what the dancer is doing." The loneliness of the choreographer is also felt in the need to create "something from virtually nothing," she says. "The dancer has to interpret and bring his or her own sensibility to the project, but he or she is not starting with nothing."

After returning from a two-month tour, Armitage recently took some time off (for the first time in ten years) and went into nature to "recharge." She hiked in Costa Rica and went cross-country skiing in Colorado. "I'm not great at it," she said, "but it really helps somehow; I'll hike for a few hours listening to music and ideas will start coming." After such hikes she returns to her hotel and record her thoughts on her iPhone.

Armitage says yoga has been very helpful in maintaining her physical being as she has aged. She practices six days a week, in a class, explaining, "It's easier to push your body in the company of others." She credits yoga with realigning her body after years of pushing it to extremes as a dancer. Unusually for a dancer, she reports not really having had any injuries: "Some aches and pains, but nothing really interesting."

A typical day in the life of Karole Armitage begins at 5 a.m. when she awakes to think about choreography. Yoga is at 7:30. At 9:30, she's off to a dance studio—whichever one she can find—where she works on phrases for the dancers to learn. If she is not working on choreography, she teaches a company class. Rehearsal is from 12:45 to 6 p.m. She described her day as "nonstop," with just one thirty-minute break for lunch. In the evening there are usually two hours of administrative work to attend to. She tries to go to bed "pretty early" (11:00 p.m.). That kind of sustained hard work has resulted in commissions to create works for the Paris Opera Ballet, the Berlin State Ballet, and Les Ballets de Monte-Carlo (the company Princess Caroline founded to honor her mother, Grace Kelly), among others.

Armitage's advice to aspiring ballet dancers is to be tenacious, and to remember there are many different kinds of dance under the overall heading of ballet. "You've got American Ballet Theatre—the traditional classical ballet, New York City Ballet (the Balanchine style), as well as a new category called 'contemporary dance,' which mixes ballet and modern. Everyone has to find their kind."

Nanette Glushak
Balanchine for the Soul

The year was 1968, and George Balanchine had come to watch a class that included 16 year-old Nanette Glushak. The very next day she was asked to join the company, on condition that she finish her last three subjects in correspondence school (she had skipped a grade and was already in her last year of high school). She was on the cusp of a long-dreamed for professional career. But her father was concerned:

> He worried that a career in dance would eventually end at an early age. He asked me what would happen if I were injured and could no longer dance. He worried that we, as dancers, had a very limited education and worked in our own world, basically locked away from 'normal' life.

Glushak came from an artistic family, so they had a sense of the struggles that might lie ahead. Her father was a frustrated artist-painter who eventually became an architect. Her mother was an accomplished violinist who was invited to be concertmaster for the Bolshoi Ballet's season at the old Metropolitan Opera House when Glushak was 3 years old. "I remember sitting with my Russian grandfather and watching *Giselle* with Galina Ulanova," she said. "That's when my obsession-possession with ballet began."

Her parents, whom she described as "completely supportive," enrolled her in violin and piano classes, but ballet was always her main objective. Her mother knew about Balanchine and the School of American Ballet, but when she called to ask about enrolling her ballet-obsessed daughter, she was advised not to begin with any form of pre-ballet, but to wait until the child was eight to start ballet lessons. "It was very difficult to wait until I was eight years old," she said.

Once she was old enough, she enrolled and studied with "all the great teachers of that era at SAB—Alexandra Danilova, Antonina Tumkovsky, Hélène Dudin, Muriel Stuart, André Eglevsky, Felia Doubrovska, Pierre Vladimirov, and of course, Stanley Williams" until the fateful day when Balanchine watched her class and offered her a spot, triggering a father's understandable concerns about the length of most dance careers. "I suppose I just detached myself from what he was saying because my love of dancing was so strong, and I had achieved my dream of dancing with Balanchine," she said. "I was able to win him over by promising that I would never stop reading." As it turned out, he needn't have worried.

After three years with New York City Ballet, Glushak moved over to American Ballet Theatre. She explained the motivation for the early move: "I was with John Prinz at the time. There had been a falling out with Mr. Balanchine. Basically for love, I followed John to ABT." But Glushak did not regret the move, in fact, she referred to this time in her career as "a great epoch." At ABT she was made a soloist, dancing numerous principal roles. Natalia Makarova became her main influence. It was the golden age at ABT with artists such as Carla Fracci, Mikhail Baryshnikov, Eric Bruhn, Rudolf Nureyev, and Sallie Wilson headlining the bill, along with a multitude of guest artists with whom Glushak would work throughout the '70s. Baryshnikov chose her as one of the muses for his first performance of *Apollo*, alongside Allegra Kent and Georgina Parkinson.

At ABT, Glushak never had time to think about the future as there were 150 performances a year. She loved every minute of every single Balanchine ballet she ever danced, while her favorite ABT roles included *Swan Lake*, *Don Quixote*, Myrtha in *Giselle*, the mistress in Tudor's *Lilac Garden* and all of Glen Tetley's ballets. She credited Tudor with being instrumental in her formation as an actress on stage, and credits her work with Tetley, Alvin Ailey and Paul Taylor in developing her more contemporary side as a dancer.

Following her departure from the company, she spent a year studying acting, singing and going to Broadway auditions (she was offered a lead in Bob Fosse's *Dancin'* but didn't take it). Then, in 1983, she received a call from Peter Martins, asking if she would be interested in going to Fort Worth, Texas where Anne Bass, a patron of NYCB, was interested in starting a school and company. Martins wanted Glushak to be the director. She had always sensed that one day she would direct a company. Before she was 30, she had started a habit of writing combinations from classes and versions of variations of the different dances. "I always had in the back of my mind that if I ever had the opportunity to improve the approach to teaching and coaching, maybe my notes would be helpful." At age 33 she accepted Martins' offer.

Glushak went on to direct the Scottish Ballet and the Ballet du Capitole in Toulouse, and says she loves teaching, coaching, and passing on what all her teachers and the artists she worked with gave her. She recognizes how fortunate she is, perhaps with an echo of her father's voice:

> Many dancers who have been forced out of a company when they begin to lose their youth, or finish their career because of a serious injury, suffer very much psychologically as they get older. I feel so lucky that I actually love my work now, as much as I loved to dance on stage. I have known many wonderful dancers—even principals—who don't have a talent to teach and are forced to work at something they're not happy with.

Glushak keeps herself in good shape into her 60's with Pilates classes every day of the year, and is forever reminding her students that it is up to them to protect, maintain and improve their bodies, along with their sense of humor. She thinks Pilates should be mandatory for all dancers starting in their teens:

> These exercises strengthen the back of the legs and the butt like no other system. These are the jumping and relevé muscles. Most dancers don't understand that relevé-pointe or demi-pointe should not be done from the calf muscles. This is where tendonitis develops. Furthermore, the upper body is too often ignored these days. Upper body exercises show clearly that if the shoulder blades are really pressed down, the stomach muscles are working automatically. None of the

exercises for the legs can be beneficial if the upper body is not placed correctly.

Glushak carries these lessons from Pilates into the studio when she teaches. She feels the upper body should not be taught separately because one part of the body cannot function without the other. When she teaches, there might be a class where she emphasizes the arms more, but the lower body always anticipates what the arms are doing. "If a dancer has not been trained to coordinate head and arms when "en dehors" they will have a particularly bad effect on the big jumps. If, for example, attention is not paid to the real efface position in a double cabriole (for the men), the landing could destroy the knees," she said.

Glushak said Natalia Makarova helped her the most with classical port de bras:

> I had a private rehearsal with her for *La Bayadère*. She devoted the entire hour to just correcting the preparation for my variation. When the hour was up, I thought, "What if I applied what she said to the technical steps as well?' And it worked! I was so much better. Although she wasn't very verbal, she demonstrated and insisted on repeating everything until we understood.

In 1987, Glushak met Michel Rahn, a former principal dancer with Ballet du Grand Théâtre de Génève. Rahn had worked with Balanchine in Geneva, so she found they spoke the same language. Rahn taught her the Vaganova method, which she calls "true pedagogy." Glushak said Rahn was one of the best teachers she has ever had. "Before meeting Michel, my teaching was pure instinct," she said. Their combined method teaches use of the upper body (following the Russian method) with the attack and musicality from the waist down (following Balanchine), and has produced and developed many professional dancers and soloists over the years. "With this combination of training, a dancer should be able to join a classical company and adapt to any choreography" she said.

Another obsession of hers is the development of artistry. For Glushak it begins in class: "Even if one is exhausted from a performance the night before, there is still a reaction in the eyes, and phrasing in the exercises at the barre when the pianist is playing a beautiful piece of music."

Glushak has been a repetiteur for the George Balanchine Trust since 1987, and is regularly invited to guest teach with many companies (primarily in Europe) as well as to stage her own versions of ballets including *Giselle* and *Don Quixote*. Of her work staging the Balanchine repertoire she said simply, "Balanchine is part of my soul."

Francia Russell

Proving You Can Have It All

At five feet, six inches tall, Francia Russell was repeatedly told she was too tall to have a professional dance career. Her years as a dancer with New York City Ballet, and three decades as founder and co-director of Pacific Northwest Ballet (with husband and former NYCB soloist Ken Stowell) are testament to the fact that sometimes it's best not to listen to the experts.

"Nowadays, five foot six is not so unusual for a ballet dancer," she said, "but back then, companies were very sensitive about hiring ballerinas over five feet four." Her first knowledgeable naysayers were the distinguished female faculty of The Sadler's Wells Ballet School (which later became the Royal Ballet School) in London. The news was delivered to her in cold, matter-of-fact fashion: "Since I was the oldest daughter of a tall father, and my toes were too long for pointe work, they said I could only do Isadora Duncan dancing. I was devastated," she said. "But it was one of the best things that ever happened to me," she added. Russell went on to study with Vera Volkova for a year whom she described as the great inspiration in her life. "She was not just an excellent teacher but the most generous person," Russell said. "She invited me to watch one-on-one coaching with some of the stars at The Royal Ballet: Margot Fonteyn, Moira Shearer, Beryl Grey, Michael Somes and David Blair."

Her training in London complete, Russell came to New York City, where Ballet Theatre was hiring girls for the corps de ballet, but Russell soon found out that Director Lucia Chase was hiring only short girls. "She told me I should give up and that I would never be a ballet dancer because I was too tall to dance," she said.

With no future at Ballet Theatre, Russell started taking classes at the School of American Ballet. Balanchine saw her and hired her two or three weeks later.

Betty Cage called and said he wanted to offer me a contract. I remember afterwards sitting on the #5 bus—I was going to my parents' house—I just wanted to get up and shout to everybody on the bus, "Mr. Balanchine just offered me a contract with the New York City Ballet!"

> Balanchine liked tall dancers, to be sure, but he also had an eye for old-world refinement, which Russell possessed. Born in Sausalito, California, she had her first ballet lesson at age seven. Her father had been an opera singer and the family went regularly to the ballet and the opera. But young Francia had no desire to be a dancer. "I was shy, and pigeon-toed. My younger sister Marilyn was the one who wanted to be a ballerina," she said. Her parents decided to enroll both girls at the San Francisco Ballet School. After three months Harold Christensen told her father, "Your oldest daughter has talent—she should continue studying."

In 1948, when Russell was 10, the family moved to Europe. Her father had always wanted to see Paris, and when he became ill, her mother urged a move. Russell continued her ballet classes in Paris until her sister got sick, prompting a move to the fresher air and warmer climate of Nice. Her father knew many of the dancers at the Ballet Russe de Monte Carlo. "There I was at age 10 or 11 taking ballet lessons with all the stars—I took a 45-minute bus ride from Nice to Monte Carlo to take private classes," she said. At 12, she was accepted into The Sadler's Wells Ballet School, sight unseen, after her father wrote a letter requesting an audition.

Russell stood in awe of Balanchine, and was eager to repay his confidence in her:

> I always felt I was in the presence of a genius. He expected us to work and work and work 24 hours a day. I used to do foot exercises to gain flexibility as I waited for the bus. He loved dancers, especially the women of course. He wanted us to be dedicated to him. We knew he was watching us all the time. He attended every performance and we were all striving to please him.

Russell found it motivating and inspiring to know that Balanchine saw his dancers as individuals, and was always alert to any changes, new capacity or progression in them. "We would notice because he would start to demand more of us," she said. She described NYCB under Balanchine as a meritocracy where one could be a member of the corps one day and a principal the next. At the same time, she recognized the downside, or the special challenge of dancing for a genius: "Ultimately, one has to take charge of one's own artistic essence and career," she said.

At 22 Russell was promoted to soloist, performing leading roles in *Western Symphony, Divertimento No. 15, Stars and Stripes, Symphony in C* and *Agon*. By 23 her performing career was over: "I had danced for a year nursing a torn meniscus and torn cartilage in my knee—I was finding it exceedingly painful to go on. Today, I could have had surgery, but there was no such thing in those days," she said. Continuing was hopeless.

For Russell, retirement brought a loss of identity. "But Balanchine was wonderful to me—he asked me to be ballet mistress," she said. Russell stayed on as a rehearsal director and taught classes until she officially retired in 1961. She was one of the first dancers at NYCB whom Balanchine chose to be a repetiteur. During a long and impressive career in that capacity, Russell traveled the world staging the ballets of her "idol/muse."

In 1977, Russell and Stowell relocated to Seattle to establish a company modeled after New York City Ballet. Over the next three decades they raised three sons, built three buildings, toured extensively, raised $10,000,000 for an endowment and built two schools. By 2005, she and Stowell felt it was time to hand over the reins, and in 2007, they retired as artistic directors of the Pacific Northwest Ballet.

Russell has found teaching and staging ballets far more satisfying than dancing ever was. She is exuberant about the opening of the Francia Russell Center, Pacific Northwest Ballet School's new home. Today, she thinks of herself not as a performer who showed great promise, but as a dedicated ballet master and teacher. "Being an exceptional dancer does not make you an exceptional teacher," she said. "So many teachers perform in class and it is all about them. The point of the class must be the student."

After a 52 year career in dance, after so many had told her she was too tall to dance, it is the influence of Balanchine—the one director who saw her as an individual—that lives on:

Each dancer is a different story. I had to be sensitive to each dancer and their emotional strengths and weaknesses. One must have the generosity of knowing when to encourage and when to be understanding.

Oleg Briansky
Forever Inspiring

More than 50 years ago, *Dance News* hailed Oleg Briansky as "the most sought-after male dancer in the world." But sadly, the title was short-lived. At age 33, Briansky was forced to retire due to a severely arthritic knee. He remembers sinking into a deep depression once he realized he would never be able to perform again. "After that, I couldn't go to a ballet performance without crying," he said, his voice becoming shaky, "I loved ballet so much. It was all I ever wanted to do."

Sitting on the sofa in his elegant apartment on Manhattan's West Side, next to his wife, former Paris Opera Ballet ballerina Mireille Briane, discussing the subsequent teaching career he has shared with her, it is clear he found his way forward. But the memories are still painful.

By the 1950s, Briansky had performed with Les Ballets des Champs Élysées, the Paris Opera Ballet, the Metropolitan Opera Ballet and the London Festival Ballet. Like many athletes and dancers, especially in an era when orthopedic medicine was less advanced, he tried to perform through his injury. "I was with the London Festival Ballet and I was in such pain that I was performing on one leg. I could dance one day and hardly walk the next," he said. Briansky went to all the doctors at that time in New York, London and Paris, but they all said there was nothing they could do.

Harold Lander, Director of the Paris Opera, offered one ray of hope, referring Briansky to a surgeon in Aarhus, Denmark. "I remember thinking, 'Why am I going to Aarhus—nobody even knows where Aarhus is,' but I sent him the X-rays from Paris, and he agreed to see me." The diagnosis was a partially torn Achilles tendon, and the doctor said he could operate. It was the first operation of its kind and the photos were published in a Danish journal of orthopedic surgery. But the doctor also wanted to take out Briansky's knee cap, and Briansky was unwilling. He rolled up his pants leg to expose the bump on his knee cap and shrugged. "Today everybody does that kind of operation," but at the time it seemed too much.

Briansky stared at the open photo album on the coffee table in front of the sofa. "I still look at these photos and I think, 'Was that me?'" The photos show Briansky partnering the world's greatest ballerinas at the time, including Violette Verdy, Alicia Markova, and Natalia Makarova. There are photos of Briansky as Mephisto, Albrecht, and Siegfried. When asked about his favorite partners, he compliments them all:

> Each ballerina was exceptional in her own style. Margot Fonteyn, Belinda Wright, Tamara Toumanova, Beryl Grey, Violette Verdy, Toni Lander… each one had something different. Toni was a

beautiful dancer. She was not a *Swan Lake* dancer, not a lyrical dancer. Makarova was a wonderfully spiritual and lyrical ballerina.

He gestured toward Ms. Brianne, his enduring partner in life and work. They are and have always been a team. It was love at first sight in Paris over 50 years ago, and they remain two of the most highly-respected teachers in the field.

The Brianskys opened their first ballet school on 91st St. and Broadway (it burned down 50 years later in an apparent arson). In 1965, the couple created the Briansky Saratoga Ballet Center at Skidmore College in upstate New York, where they remained for 43 years. In April of 2010, they relocated their summer program from Skidmore to the campus of Mount Holyoke in South Hadley, Massachusetts. Although the Brianskys are no longer teaching class, they remain very much in the center of things at their school.

"We see so many students who come to us and haven't the faintest idea of what they're doing," Briansky said. "They are always struggling and often ready to give up. We give them confidence in themselves." The Brianskys view their role as supplementing the students' overall education. "For example, schools don't tell students how to sit at a table," he said, "to sit straight so you don't slouch—that's a kind of discipline."

The couple have had their share of exceptional students, including principal dancers with San Francisco Ballet, the Paris Opera Ballet and the Boston Ballet. "Of course ballet is not for everybody," Briansky said. "Many come and want to be ballerinas but few are chosen." Other students went away with valuable life lessons. Briansky recounted one example:

> One student, who is now a drama coach, communicated with us recently. She said, "I remember my session with you at Skidmore College years ago. I never forgot what your guidelines were, not just for dancing, but for being a human being—accepting life...the difficulties...the struggle. The precepts you taught me as a young girl, I now apply to my students."

Another student in the Skidmore program returned recently to tell the couple, "I'll always remember how you took care of me when I was 10 years old, when I was away from my parents. You gave me so much love and care. I have never forgotten." Briansky glanced at his wife, "At least we are useful. We always wanted to do something in life where we could be useful."

Briansky says the greatest challenge of teaching is to instill confidence. Once students have mastered certain steps and combinations, they can begin to acquire a sense of style:

> ...to be able to convey to the audience that you are not just an empty soul, but that you are human. Ballet technique has advanced so much, but there is technique and then there is *artistry*. You may do 12 pirouettes but if it doesn't have the artistry....We have always tried to make our students artists.

Like dancing, Briansky says teaching is essentially a gift. "Not every principal dancer is a good teacher," he said, and conversely, he has seen good teachers who never really danced. "Many principal dancers who turn to teaching after they stop performing learn on the job," he said. "At first, they rely on the teaching of their masters to know what to do, but, gradually, they find their own method, which grows and develops and they become good and inspiring teachers." Briansky added, "It requires insight, to feel the approach."

At this point in life, Briansky no longer thinks of himself as a dancer. He stared reflectively at the photo albums of his meteoric performing career:

> As you age, you reject things, so I tell myself, "This was the past." It was a good past. This was a phase of my life which I was very happy to have because I was successful and recognized. But life goes on. You have to face reality. I have had very few options aside from dancing and teaching but I will say this: when you see how a student's body develops and acquires technique, it is very rewarding for a teacher. It is like planting a seed and watching it grow, and then you see the result!

Today Briansky looks around and sees teachers of his age or even younger seeking retirement, because of "the strenuous physical nature of what we do," but says he has never contemplated it. Ms. Briane interjected, "Retirement means you stop doing what you're doing. If you stop doing, you're dead." After more than 50 years of teaching, Briansky vows he won't retire. "It's against my religion."

Gemze de Lappe (1922 - 2017)
Handing Down the Past

"Sing, sing, sing, sing / Everybody start to sing"—strains of the Benny Goodman favorite resounded from somewhere within the walls of Gemze de Lappe's Upper West Side apartment in Manhattan. De Lappe excused herself, got up and left the living room to answer her cell phone. "Where are you?" came her voice from the next room. "So, when will you get here?...Oh, wonderful!... Good, I'm kind of booked for the next few days...I can't wait to see you...Bye." She came rushing back, apologizing for the interruption and settled into her favorite upholstered oak chair. At age 94, there was nothing to indicate this dance icon had slowed down a bit.

Over the years, her name has become synonymous with staging the works of Agnes de Mille, including the iconic *Rodeo, Fall River Legend, Oklahoma!, Carousel,* and *Paint Your Wagon,* to name a few. De Lappe, who referred to de Mille as "revolutionary for her time," recreated de Mille's choreography for theater and ballet companies, universities and educational institutions throughout the world.

During her long and distinguished career, she choreographed some 50 ballets, shows and concerts. She staged *The King and I* from the original choreography and did her own staging for a number of other shows, including *Camelot*.

Whether she was reconstructing de Mille's choreography, choreographing herself, or coaching for major ballet companies, when de Lappe worked, the floor was hers alone. The passion, devotion, and commitment were always there. She was equally fascinating on stage and off.

Throughout her career, the age-defying de Lappe was the recipient of various honors and awards including the Tony Honors for Excellence in Theater in 2007, and, along with Yuriko Kikuchi, the 2012 Lifetime Achievement Award presented by the Martha Hill Dance Fund.

De Lappe was born in Virginia in 1922. Her father was a World War I vet, an engineer and designer by profession. Her mother did some folk dancing and a little ballet. At a time when it was not the norm for women to leave home to start a career elsewhere, her mother did just that at 18 to play the drums with the Women's Symphony Orchestra in Denver. It was this kind of independence that de Lappe said explains her own subsequent career determination. "It's in the DNA," she said.

When de Lappe was three, the family moved to Baltimore where she studied violin and piano as well as ballet with Gertrude Coburn, who taught what is known as "plastique ballet," a common name given to ballet based on the Cecchetti method.

When she was nine, the family relocated to New York where she later enrolled in the Ballet Arts School. She also studied with Irma Duncan, one of Isadora Duncan's seven adopted daughters, who taught at the Broadway Central Hotel in Manhattan. There she caught the eye of choreographer Michel Fokine, who visited one of the recitals. He offered her a scholarship to his school, which was housed in a huge mansion on 73rd Street and Riverside Drive, where she was one of five female students between the ages of eight and nine.

De Lappe danced with the Fokine Ballet, a company made up mostly of dancers who had migrated to New York, between the ages of 9 and 15. "I became a professional," she said. The Fokine Ballet performed on Randall's Island where such shows as *Anything Goes, Roberta*, and *Of Thee I Sing* were being performed every week. "It was marvelous. There is nothing like dancing all day and performing at night. I was in heaven and I got $25 a week."

Although she was not in the original production of *Oklahoma!*, she traveled to London with the national company. The year was 1947, and it was the first time the British Actors' Equity Association had allowed a foreign company to come and perform. De Lappe was the only one in the show familiar with the choreography in its entirety, so the Theatre Guild and Rodgers and Hammerstein said she could assist the director. She was put in charge of bringing a new cast of actors, singers and dancers up to speed. "That's where I learned my job—at the Drury Lane," said de Lappe. De Lappe recalled an early, important lesson from choreographer/director Michael Kidd:

> Shortly after we arrived in London, Michael Kidd, whom I had known socially in New York, came to do *Finian's Rainbow*. We were free all day so I had a chance to come over and watch him hold an audition. It was a revelation to me. Being so nervous myself, I hadn't really faced up to the fact that it was my job to make the cast more comfortable. When I watched Michael, I saw how humorous he was with them. There was an exchange of conversation instead of his being distant and remote. Thanks to Michael, I learned not to be critical of the performers, but to help them to show their best.

De Lappe acknowledges there is less demand today for the original choreography for shows from the golden era of musicals:

> Today's companies don't really do the golden era—the '40s, '50s, and '60s—and *when* they do them, they try to improve on them, which is not helpful. They come up with all sorts of wacky ideas to make them more up-to-date. On the other hand, while there is less of a demand for the original choreography, there are certain companies that do it, and they want Agnes' choreography to be as close as possible to the way the show was originally done.

She stared out the window, "There were three shows done with international companies 10 or 15 years ago that just went off the deep end in various ways, so Rodgers and Hammerstein decided they didn't want that to happen anymore. They tried to control it as much as they could." She laughed. "There was one production of *The King and I* in which the first time you see the king, he is sitting like King Tut." She demonstrated a pose with remarkable agility. "The corps of golden-clad dancers looked as though they were in Las Vegas instead of the library scene. The king was a scholar. That was the king that Oscar Hammerstein tried to historically keep as accurately as possible."

De Lappe always loved acting. When she spent two years as a soloist with Ballet Theatre between 1953 and 1955, she did only actor-dancer parts including the girl in *Fancy Free* who does the pas de deux. "It was all acting through and through and it seemed like a natural thing for me to do," she said. After leaving Ballet Theatre to join Agnes de Mille's company, her demanding career continued to draw on her acting skills. She recalled her return to Ballet Theatre, now American Ballet Theatre, to coach ballerinas Gillian Murphy and Julie Kent in de Mille's *Fall River Legend*:

In addition to learning the steps, *Fall River Legend* involves a lot of acting. It's a lot of material to absorb in a forty-minute ballet. Gillian wanted to work on the acting so I taught her what I had done with the role. We went to the stage, to the scenery where I could show her. The house was standing there by itself – empty. Believe me, it's not easy to dive into a drama like *Fall River Legend* on a Sunday morning in your street clothes. I slammed the door open and came in panting. If you'd hacked your parents forty whacks, you'd be on a big high. I went through the whole thing, which was quite different from the way it was staged, But I hadn't changed anything—it was all in the acting. When Gillian did it in performance, she got all the kudos she deserved.

After marriage at 38 and the birth of her two sons, de Lappe's career slowed, but never stopped. She performed intermittently on TV, including the role of the dance hall girl in a ballet called "Gold Rush" from *Paint Your Wagon,* a role that re-established her reputation as one of the best actor-dancers around. Many consider it the signature role of her performing career. She was Simon Legree in *The King and I* on Broadway for six months in 1951. She pointed to a picture of herself on the wall. "I've shrunk three inches since." Although she repeated her show-stopping performance in the film version, she was not given screen credit, something she always felt disappointed about. When Jerome Robbins started rehearsing the movie at 20th Century Fox, de Lappe was performing in Europe, but upon her return to New York, he sent for her. The movie had been in rehearsal for four weeks and she had only one week to rehearse. She was ultimately only given credit for a "specialty dance."

Well into her 40's, while raising her two sons, de Lappe continued to perform on Broadway as well as at City Center and Lincoln Center in *Carousel, Kismet and Brigadoon*. In the fall of 1979, de Lappe was hired by Smith College to teach musical theater. "I didn't know if I would like it," she said, "but I did and they liked me." She stayed for ten years, finding satisfaction in mentoring young dancers and giving back to her craft.

As for the qualities she looks for in a young dancer she said, "The first thing I look for is the passion to do it, and if they can make an intelligent connection with what they are trying to do. I never discourage a student when they don't look promising. By the time they are college-aged, you can encourage them to explore other aspects of dance, for example, folk dancing or ethnic dancing."

While acknowledging that ageing takes its toll on the body, no matter how flexible or strong we may be, she believes that once you're a dancer, you're always a dancer. Surprisingly, she incurred few injuries during her career. The only accident she could recall occurred one winter when she fell on the ice in front of her New York City apartment house, injuring her knee.

When de Lappe could not attend class regularly, she would warm up using the kitchen sink or her heavy oak living room chair for support. Her routine included fondus, passés, developpés and grand battements. The morning news provided her accompaniment. At night, it was the music on WQXR. Of her exercise routine in her 90's de Lappe said, "I still warm up if I force myself, although the last couple of years, I find it harder. But you've got to keep moving." She paused, "That's another advantage to being with a big company—you can go take a barre every day."

So what is it about the original choreography of ballets that makes them so valuable in today's world of contemporary dance? As one of the people most responsible for keeping alive some of the greatest works of 20th century American dance, de Lappe makes a strong case:

> If you're going to do a period piece, it's important to put the performers in the right clothing with the right music and the right choreography. When you talk about production, it's not just dance. It's the style of the show, it's music, it's everything. No one would dream of performing *Oklahoma!* and changing Rodgers and Hammerstein's music and lyrics. Why change the dance? When it is done properly, it's not dated. These people—the writer, the choreographer, the director—all worked together as one tightly-collaborated unit. It's hard to improve on what these geniuses have done.

Ted Kivitt

Carrying on the Torch

When Ted Kivitt looks in the mirror these days, he no longer sees the much sought-after American Ballet Theatre principal dancer of the '60s and '70s. Rather, he sees a much sought-after teacher on the faculty of the dance department at Purchase College. I caught up with Kivitt relaxing in his office in the Dance Building. "What I do now is exciting because there is a lot of talent out there and so much competition in the real world. What we do here is educate them in a college atmosphere and then they can go out and get jobs," said Kivitt.

Kivitt, along with his wife, Michelle Lucci, former principal dancer with Milwaukee Ballet, make the 20-minute commute to Purchase from their Riverdale condominium every day. "Hopefully, we can give these students the best education here because we are basically modern-ballet, not ballet-modern. The ballet helps the modern," said Kivitt. "I was hoping we would have a two-track system, but I don't think that is going to happen. But to be in the school, you have to have a very strong ballet foundation."

At auditions Kivitt looks first for students who are smart. He checks their GPA. When auditioning throughout the country, he looks for body types – the feet, the legs, the whole instrument. "If the facility is not there, they are injured all the time," said Kivitt. He also looks for how the dancers express themselves through movement. He does not like to see a "cold" dancer. And he looks for entertainment qualities. "You want to sell the audience. I always remind them they are entertainers."

Kivitt comes from a family of artists and entertainers. One uncle, Russ Brown, was in the original Broadway cast of *Damn Yankees*. Another relative was the award-winning playwright Arthur Miller. Kivitt described his family as very supportive. His father was a policeman with a beautiful voice who always wanted to be a singer. His mother was a musician who had also been a tap dancer, but she loved ballet and would go all the time. Both parents were of European extraction and the family had many horror stories of the WWII. His paternal grandparents were able to flee to Argentina where his grandfather worked for his great grandfather on a cattle ranch. Eventually, they migrated to New York.

Kivitt began dancing at age 7, with tap and gymnastics. He described himself as "a really hyper little kid, always dancing around the house." He and his brother loved Gene Kelly and Fred Astaire. "We would entertain at family gatherings. My mother wanted me to have a way to release my energy and she thought, 'well maybe dancing.'" Growing up with asthma, Kivitt was sick through much of his childhood, "coughing, spitting up blood," but unlike many asthmatics, dance and exercise seemed to help him. "Dancing seemed to inhabit my body," said Kivitt. "Every time I heard music, I would move with the music."

Kivitt did not see his first ballet until age ten, after he had started ballet training with Alexander Garault in Miami, Florida, who was a friend of Nijinsky. What he saw, like so many young dancers of that era, was the touring company of Ballet Russe de Monte Carlo, starring Alicia Alonso and Igor Youskevitch in *Giselle*. "Little did I know I would be working with them one day," said Kivitt. He still remembers the day vividly: "My mother purchased a ticket for me. It was breathtaking. I couldn't believe Youskevitch's dancing and the beauty of Alonso and the set, the magic, the beautiful music—it all came together."

Thomas Armour, a local ballet teacher who had been with the Ballet Russe and had a lot of friends in the company, was there when Kivitt's mother picked him up, and offered to give Kivitt a tour backstage after the performance. It was Kivitt's first taste of backstage life. Kivitt continued, "The smell of makeup, the sweat, and all the beautiful people. I said, 'Oh my God! This is what I want to do.'" When Kivitt returned home that night he announced that he wanted to be a ballet dancer. "And I stuck to it," said Kivitt.

Kivitt initially took private lessons because he was so shy. At age 12, Armour became his teacher after Garault died, then Georges Milenoff. His performance career got off to an early start. At 14, while in the ninth grade, he was hired by Lou Walters (father of Barbara Walters) to be the lead male dancer at his Miami Beach night club. "I lied. I said I was 18," said Kivitt. He did it all: tap, jazz, ballet. When his grades began to fall, he left regular school and put himself through professional private school. "My family had banked my allowance, so I had the money to do it," he said. School didn't start until noon, so he could sleep in after late nights dancing at the club. He did his homework in his dressing room.

To his early performing career, Kivitt soon added an early teaching career. "At the nightclub, they were looking for somebody to teach a class. Everybody had had some ballet training so I said I'd give a class to the first show and a warm-up class to the second show," he said. "My whole life was always about doing the most difficult thing I could possibly do."

When Kivitt was 16, ABT was appearing in Miami and Armour arranged for him to take a company class. After the class, Kivitt was approached by Director Lucia Chase, who invited him to come back the following night for another class. Enrique Martinez, Dimitri Romanoff, Freddie Franklin, and Oliver Smith were there along with Chase. After taking company class for two weeks, he was invited to join ABT. He had received offers from other companies, but had been told to hold out for ABT. He joined right after he attended his school graduation wearing his Bermuda shorts on Miami Beach.

At ABT he excelled in ballets which featured gymnastics. "I could jump like a kangaroo," he said. "That's how I got to do all the technical male roles." At ABT, his biggest idols were Royes Fernandez, whom he called "the epitome of a classical dancer," Lupe Serrano, and Toni Lander. "They all helped me along the way," he said. "One thing that was so great about ABT was that there was no jealousy. It could have been there, but maybe I was so naïve I didn't see it," he added.

He was also known for his thoughtful partnering. "It's all about the ballerina," he said. When partnering, Kivitt took the approach that he had his time, his solos, but once he was in back of the ballerina, "you partner her to always make her look good no matter what." Being able to adapt to the moment is also key: "When the ballerina needs help or when something is happening on stage, you can change it or fix it because you know the music so well." Of his partnership with Carla Fracci, Kivitt said, "A lot of the time I would just feed off of her. When we did *Giselle*, the first act was different every time, which made it exciting."

Kivitt tells his students to approach partnering like a marriage:

Partnering is the two of you looking into each other's eyes and knowing what is going to happen next. You learn to get along with each other, to listen to each other. You know when something is wrong.

When Kivitt was in his late 30s, he became aware that he had started putting on weight even though he was working just as hard. He started to lose the power that he had had when he was younger. He felt his strength was waning. Exhausted after finishing a pas de deux, he would go into his dressing room and just sit there and stare at the wall.

Things were also changing at ABT. The company had begun to hire many international guest artists who were now dancing the principal roles when the company performed in New York City. Natalia Makarova defected from the Soviet Union and was hired by ABT as a guest artist. Makarova was followed by Baryshnikov. Kivitt, along with several other American dancers, protested to no avail:

> I was brought up in a generation where I would do two or three ballets a night. This was no longer true. We would be cast when we went on the road on one-night stands, but when we got back to New York we were not cast as we had been. ABT was bringing the international artists into New York because they were big box office draws. They were the principals who helped make the company during my generation. I guess I was upset about what was happening.

Kivitt was up for a new contract and remembered telling Lucia Chase it was time for him to leave. "I told Lucia I didn't want to be a hanger on—I didn't want to go out looking bad. I wanted to be remembered at the top of my profession." He finally quit ABT in 1979.

His spectacular journey with ABT, with Lucia Chase at the helm, had taken him from the corps de ballet to principal dancer. "Dear Lucia, she was like my mother, I loved her," he said. He remembered when he and Cynthia Gregory were promoted to principal dancers. "There was a huge article in Dance Magazine. I saved every article." He corrected himself, "Well actually, it was my mother who saved every article that was ever written about me."

Kivitt's love of performance, the respectful way he approached it, and a certain feeling of nostalgia for his days on the stage still hang over him:

> I think I will always miss that time walking from the shadows of the wings into the lights and transforming myself into whatever character I was performing. Going from the dark into the light was unbelievable to me—I really miss that—that and getting ready for a performance. I used to go over to the Met and lie down right in the middle of the stage and go over the choreography and the feelings of *Swan Lake*, for example. I would listen to the music of every role and play it before I went to sleep and learn every note so I knew every nuance and all the counts. Lucia had instilled in me that you're only as good as your last performance. You had to be the best every time because the audience was paying to see you perform. I never forgot that.

Kivitt did not consciously plan for a career transition. Having enjoyed an international reputation, he had done frequent guest appearances all over the world, starting in 1969, with Lupe Serrano at the University of Milwaukee dance department. There was a dream to get a company started, and it began with college students putting on performances at the university. Kivitt approached many of his colleagues at ABT, who all donated their services to raise funds to help keep the Milwaukee company going.

This early interest and support for dance in an academic setting truly flowered once Kivitt retired from the stage and joined the staff at SUNY Purchase, as a professor of dance. In addition, he was founding director of Dance/USA, and was one of the adjudicators for the National Endowment for the Arts, where he learned about funding.

As a guest artist travelling around the country, Kivitt has seen many students receiving poor training and bemoans the fact that most parents do not know what a good teacher is. "Parents are taking a risk when they place their children in the hands of a teacher. Many go on pointe too early before the bones are fully formed and set themselves up for disaster later on." He believes schools and teachers should be licensed, and is working on creation of a standard syllabus so schools know what to teach. "You can get a license for this or that thing, but you don't get a license to teach dance?" he questioned. "American Ballet Theatre is doing that right now. They are offering teaching classes for schools throughout the country. Teachers have to pass a test and they receive a certificate. As a result, we're seeing better and better dancers."

Kivitt believes that students should start studying ballet at about age ten, once the brain is more formed and students can understand it more. "You can go and hold an audition and many students will allude to the fact that they've had 15 years of ballet training." Of even greater importance is that students be taught correctly at the beginning stages. "Once they learn the movement incorrectly, it is almost impossible to fix it unless they will take the time to go into a studio and work on their own."

Now in his 70s, Kivitt said, "I'm proud of my age. I'm in pretty good shape." He has never engaged in any other occupation but dance. "I've been lucky," he acknowledged, "I've never had to wait on tables or do other odd jobs. I always went from one dance job to the next."

Ann Reinking
Staying True to Herself

Three little swans danced in the playground, and one of them grew up to possess the best pins in the business. Ann Reinking described her first encounter with ballet, when she was 11:

> The school had a talent show. One girl was already en pointe and she did the Sugar Plum Fairy from *The Nutcracker*. I had never seen anything like that and I asked her what it was — I knew right away that was what I wanted to do. So, she and another girl, who also took ballet, showed me the Dance of the Four Little Swans from *Swan Lake* on the playground."

Reinking remembers taking naturally to the schoolyard choreography. "I didn't think about it at all, I just did it. Sometimes to be innocent makes it easier," she said. She went home and auditioned her newfound talent for her family. "They said if I could do that, I should be taking ballet lessons. Those girls gave me my life. Actually, there's a long list, but it started with them."

Reinking began ballet lessons in her hometown of Seattle, with Marian and Illaria Ladré. She credits them for teaching not only ballet, but an aesthetic that set her on a path: "They had performed in costumes by Coco Chanel with the Ballet Russe. I realized years later they taught me manners, amazing life skills, and all that history."

The first fully professionally-produced ballet she attended was The Royal Ballet with Margot Fonteyn and Michael Somes. "It was magic and I cried," she said. In 1967, after high school, she moved to New York where she received a scholarship for a month to study with The Joffrey Ballet School, where Robert Joffrey nudged her toward the footlights of Broadway. She auditioned for Radio City Music Hall and was hired two weeks later.

From there her Broadway career took off. She went on the road with *Fiddler on the Roof*, and got her equity card. Then came an offer to be in the chorus of *Cabaret* for the final three months of its Broadway run. "The closing notice was already up, but I said I'd do it," she said. The decision proved to be a good one. The dance captain referred Reinking to Michael Bennett, the choreographer for *Coco*, starring Katharine Hepburn. *Coco* was followed by *Wild and Wonderful* and *Pippin*. She received the Theatre World Award for her portrayal of Maggie in *Over Here, and Drama Desk* and Tony Award nominations (Best Actress in a Musical) for *Goodtime Charley*, which was followed by starring roles in *A Chorus Line* and *Chicago* where she originated the role of Roxie Hart. She was also nominated for a Tony in Bob Fosse's *Dancin'*. After a stint in Hollywood, including a role in Fosse's *All That Jazz*, she returned to Broadway to star in *Sweet Charity* in 1986. Reinking was both muse and lover to Fosse, and she came to define the Fosse style:

> You can always recognize Fosse's choreography. Whatever he choreographed, it could be edgy, but it never looked lurid. He never crossed the line. It always had elegance. He had a phrase, "soft-boiled egg hands—no shell." You caress

> the egg with your hands. He used it in the frug in *Sweet Charity*. You put your arms back—it's a reverse *Swan Lake* port de bras, and a beautiful image. That's what gives it its fragile strength.

In the decades that followed, Reinking came into her own as a choreographer, teacher, actress, and director. She appeared in six films, including *All that Jazz*. Of her role in the film, which is said to be loosely based on Fosse's life, Reinking said, "I just didn't want to let Bob down. I trusted that he wouldn't want to do anything in the film that would offend anybody. I didn't feel intruded upon. Katie was a character, like me."

Reinking spoke highly of her co-star in the film, Roy Scheider, who played the Fosse-like character:

> Roy was wonderful. His ability to imitate was extraordinary. He followed Bob around, and after a while, it was hard to tell the difference between Bob and Roy. He wasn't a dancer, but I got to tell you, he knew all the language, and what the names of the moves were, and could put together a ballet combination on his own and repeat it across the floor. He was very comfortable partnering, and Bob used that in the film. Roy always put me down right in my center. He had a marvelous sense of leverage and balance. He was always fit, and practiced yoga for many years, giving him grace, fluidity and a strong sense of line. He was very well-coordinated. He loved baseball, so Bob used baseball slides for Roy to do many times in the final number called "Bye Bye Life."

Reinking feels that what the film had to say was deeper than what most people thought. "The film did two things: it was very entertaining and artful, and it also had a message," she said. Of the pill popping scenes in the film, she says that was not like Fosse at all, and that he knew he was risking his reputation by including them in a film based loosely on his life. "There were artistic liberties and choices made for the story—those scenes were added because they fit the character, not because they were autobiographical," she said. She once asked Fosse why he included those scenes, since he was not addictive like Joe Gideon. He told her he did not want to construct Joe Gideon too autobiographically because he wanted the audience to better embrace the point of the film: that narcissism and glamour can be very dangerous, even fatal. "When he told me that, I was even more committed to the project. He made a sacrifice whether he knew it or not," said Reinking.

Fosse died in 1987. "He had so many wonderful qualities," she said. Reinking described Fosse's huge contribution to the dance world:

> He made dance equally as important as singing and acting in a musical. He helped to bring about the "triple threat" which is someone who can do all three disciplines. He also created a very special dance style that was instantly recognizable, like the way Balanchine's style is instantly recognizable.

Over the years, Reinking has choreographed for major ballet companies, for TV, and for theaters around the country. In 1996, she returned to Broadway, to reprise her role as Roxie Hart in *Chicago*. She described how her portrayal differed at age 46:

> I felt Roxie's desperation so much more than the first time I did the role. Because I was more of a woman, it automatically informed the character. This is Roxie's last chance. It is Roxie's need to capture her dreams. If she doesn't make it now, she never will.

Obviously age brought challenges as well. "'Me and My Baby,' is technically very aerobic," she said. "The composer/lyricist team, Kander and Ebb, asked if I'd go back to the original arrangement. I kept it very aerobic and injured my back" (she had fractured her back early in her career when she was in her 20s). "Injuries like that will come back," she said. "Growing old is not for sissies," she said, quoting Bette Davis. At one point, she lost all feeling in her legs and was out for a month. She described her return:

> I couldn't do anything like a 90-degree arabesque or a stag leap, and I had always been a very good jumper. I had to rechoreograph the number. It was still Fosse's vocabulary. But there are many ways of saying the same thing, and they can work at any age. You have to be the judge. Sometimes, necessity is the mother of invention.

Reinking was well-acquainted with injury throughout her career: the broken back (fractured vertebrae in two places on T-12), torn hamstrings, torn calf muscle, stripped Achilles tendons, numerous ankle sprains, a concussion, a broken hand, a pulled groin, and an injured left knee. In her mid-30s, she began to see that she would not be able to continue doing everything she was used to doing, from a technique standpoint. In her mid-40s, she started making adjustments. The biggest changes came in her 50s:

> It was discovered I had a hole in my heart, and my heart was also enlarged. It's been taken care of thanks to brilliant science, but I'm a different person. I had to accommodate. Spins are different—I had to slow it down and use less energy and try to synchronize balance and spotting. It's a big adjustment, and humbling. At least spins can still be part of one's dance language.

Far from retired, the last few years have seen Reinking increase her choreographic endeavors, including two story ballets, *White City*, adapted from a book *Devil and the White City*, and *A Light in the Dark*, about Helen Keller and Annie Sullivan, for Thodos Dance Chicago. She was Executive Producer of the documentary *In My Hands: A Story of Marfan Syndrome*, about the genetic disease of the connective tissue that afflicts her son. "It's very close to my heart," she said. The documentary depicts Reinking's efforts to contradict negative body image by choreographing dances designed to highlight the body differences (unusually long arms and legs) of those with Marfan Syndrome, showing the beauty of being different.

Looking back on her career, she says she is happy with all her choices, which she feels were right for her and for the people she loved:

> I wanted a family, and I wanted to perform, and sometimes one has to choose. But I did dance, I danced a lot, and that makes me feel very good and blessed. It is a privilege to be able to dance. But I don't think I could work without being humanized by my love, friendships, and compassion, and what it takes to maintain the ups and downs of lifetime relationships. Life is another art form. The choices I made informed my dancing. But I don't think you can devote your life to dance unless you are incredibly, compassionately, in love with it. Passion is definitely a must! It's a constant juggle between your personal life and dance.

Reinking has this advice for today's youngsters who want to make dancing a career:

> Along with your training, be sure to understand the psychology of being in the theater, how to handle rejection, anger, narcissism, how to handle finding jobs, how to make adjustments, sometimes over and over, and always remember it's supposed to be fun! This is a beautiful art form and you must love it, I mean truly love it because if you don't, it will just be too hard. You must have other things in your life: family, friends, other art forms, sports, whatever you really like, and commit to those things as well, because the mix will be a buffer for all the ups and downs.

When asked what was the strangest thing that ever happened in her career, she recalled the many script changes during the previews of *Goodtime Charley*:

> In the scene that closed the first act, there were script changes made every evening. Because there were so many, in most cases, small changes, one night, I did the Wednesday script, Joel Grey did the Thursday script, and the rest of the cast did the Friday script. Fortunately, it all made sense. The audience never knew.

And the most valuable advice she ever received? Reinking recounted the time when her teacher in Seattle, Gwen Barker, urged her to call Ruthana Boris, who was head of the University of Washington's dance department at the time:

I was very nervous and kept stammering. Boris was a very straightforward woman. She asked me if I was any good. All I could do was flounder and stammer, and then she said, "When someone asks you if you are any good, you better find out. You've got to answer that truthfully." There's a humble strength in that good advice: "Know Thyself."

Louis Johnson (1930-2020)

Pushing the Envelope

In 1952, Jerome Robbins took notice of an upcoming talent: Louis Johnson, one of the first black students at the School of American Ballet. Robbins not only invited Johnson to guest with New York City Ballet, but featured him as a principal dancer in *Ballade*, alongside five white NYCB dancers. But Johnson was never invited to join the company. Unfortunately, neither the company nor the country was quite ready for a black ballet dancer (Raven Wilkinson would break the color barrier in 1955 with the Ballet Russe de Monte Carlo, while Arthur Mitchell joined NYCB the same year. In 1957 Mitchell, as a principal dancer, would dance *Agon* with a white ballerina, Diana Adams, to rave reviews).

Interviewed at his New York City apartment, where he was confined to a wheelchair and waiting for a hip operation, Johnson spoke candidly about his early days in New York—the well-deserved successes and the difficult challenges. He had come up through SAB in the company of such New York City Ballet luminaries as Nora Kaye, Tanaquil Le Clercq and Janet Reed. But classical ballet didn't offer him a home.

Johnson recalled Robbins as being very encouraging and kind to him, even offering him work as a housekeeper to help ends meet. But no amount of talent or hard work would allow Johnson to break the color barrier in ballet at that time. Eventually, he was forced to widen the field for himself, turning to Broadway and then Hollywood, before starting his own company. "Those days everybody formed a company," Johnson said. He was director, choreographer and star. His signature role was "Harlequin," featuring the acrobatic choreography he had always excelled in. "I called myself a jazz-modern-ballet dancer. There were about six or seven people in the company—we did everything."

Johnson did not always want to dance. As a youngster, he was on the acrobatics team at the local YMCA in Washington D.C. When he was 14, dance teachers Doris Jones and Clara Haywood saw him perform and offered him a scholarship to their ballet school, which Haywood had founded and funded to offer African-American youngsters the chance to study classical dance. Johnson cleaned their apartment to help defray his living expenses. When asked if he remembered the very moment he decided to become a dancer, he replied, "I never decided to become a dancer. Clara and Doris decided for me."

Impressed with his talent, two years later, Haywood took Johnson, along with another promising student, Chita Rivera, to audition for Balanchine. Johnson remembered how excited he was at just the thought of the audition. "He was George Balanchine—just to be auditioning for him alone was an incredible experience." Rivera and Johnson were auditioned in a separate studio from the white students, and both received scholarships to SAB.

Johnson's stage career was studded with appearances in such hit musicals as *House of Flowers, Kwamina, My Darlin' Aida*, and *Hallelujah, Baby!* He performed in both the film and stage versions of *Damn Yankees*. Alluding to the stage version, Johnson laughed, saying, "I was their Jackie Robinson. I was the only African-American in the cast, and I was in it for two years."

At age 40, he stopped performing to focus on his choreography. The first ballet he choreographed for his company was *Lament,* performed at the 92nd St. Y. Johnson would go on to choreograph works for Alvin Ailey American Dance Theater, Dance Theatre of Harlem, and the Metropolitan Opera. His choreographic credits included *Treemonisha,* and the revivals of *Purlie* (for which he was nominated for a Tony award) and *Lost in the Stars*. He was creative consultant to an original musical, *Play On!,* and he choreographed the film version of *The Wiz* and the film *Cotton Comes to Harlem*. He never missed the applause he received while dancing, instead he said he "wanted the applause for my choreography."

Through the 1980s he was a prolific arts educator and teacher, notably conducting black arts symposiums at educational institutions throughout the country, including Yale, Virginia State, and Morehouse College.

At the time of our interview, Johnson said he no longer stayed in touch with the dance world. "But I always watch dance on television," he said. "I just love sitting and watching all those good old MGM Technicolor musicals." He paused thoughtfully. "I still do dance," he said. "I dance in my mind and I dance in my heart."

Marcello Angelini

Unstoppable

D ance "was something ingrained in my DNA," explained Marcello Angelini, artistic director of the Tulsa Ballet:

> My father was a dancer when I was born. At that time, he was working for a touring company. They tell stories that as early as six months, I was sitting in the wings with whatever dancer was off that night and watching the shows. We would travel from city to city in a small Fiat 500, the old ones, and lived in bed and breakfasts for years. By age three, I was apparently left alone in the first wing of the theaters and watched the shows by myself. Unfortunately, I have no recollection of that time.

When he was six, his father won an audition for a life contract to the Teatro di San Carlo and the family settled down in Naples, Italy. His mother, whom he described as in many ways the opposite of his dad, was a bookkeeper who stopped working when Angelini was born. His younger brother was also a dancer and teacher with a lifetime contract at San Carlo. But Angelini's early years at the Teatro di San Carlo Ballet School were not promising:

> We all get into dance because we want to dance, but the process of going from zero to being able to do what we see on stage takes an agonizing eight years. I remember that by my third year in ballet school, I was terribly bored. I wanted to dance, and all we did were very slow exercises at the barre. When we are very young, we don't understand the importance of learning and honing the basic principles that eventually become the foundation of our technique.

At the end of his third year, he was told he would never be good enough to be in the corps. The insult stung:

> I will admit that I might not have been the most engaged student in the class, but saying that I didn't have the talent to join the corps? Thankfully, my dad thought otherwise and took me into his school, but not before I threw a fit and told the director that I would come back to the theater as a big star one day and charge them a small fortune.

Five years later, after graduating from his father's school, he auditioned for the company of the Teatro Comunale di Bologna. One day he was having coffee with his father in the main square of the city when an old acquaintance of his dad, a former dancer at the San Carlo, happened to walk by. He joined them for coffee, and when he got up to leave, he said, "By the way, do you know that there is an audition in Florence tomorrow?" Angelini changed his travel plans and the next day auditioned for the Maggio Musicale Fiorentino, a company considered second only to La Scala at that time in Italy.

Maggio Musicale Fiorentino was run by Evgeny Polyakov (who later became assistant to Rudolf Nureyev at the Paris Opera Ballet), and Angelini and his wife Daniella were both offered contracts, becoming two of Polyakov's pet projects. The master took the Angelinis under his wing, working with them and two other couples during every break from the company's schedule for three years. Angelini described the special mentoring relationship:

> He taught us the classical repertory, found performances outside the theater where we could perform it, and then started casting us as second casts to the big stars that came as guests in the main theater. We owe him a lot.

Polyakov encouraged Angelini to apply for a special government scholarship, awarded to two young Italian dancers every year, to study in the former Soviet Union. Angelini applied "just for fun," was awarded the scholarship, and spent a year in Kiev honing his skills. After graduation, he returned to Florence to continue working with Polyakov, before moving on to Berlin, where the Angelinis were offered soloist contracts at the Deutsche Oper Berlin. Things didn't exactly click for them in Berlin. "Our Italian temperaments, kind of open and sunny, didn't fit well with the Berlin personalities," he explained. They left after a year and auditioned for the London Festival Ballet (now English National Ballet).

While John Field, the artistic director of the company, liked them very much, there were no vacancies in the company at the time, so Field arranged for them to audition and join the Northern Ballet, directed by Robert de Warren, while they waited for positions to open. At the Northern they were offered principal contracts and decided to stay for three years. "We did between 220 and 240 performances a year. The repertoire was great, and we had Nureyev dancing with us for three or four months every season," said Angelini. He alternated with Nureyev in all the leading roles, and soon the Angelinis were being invited to guest at various opera houses in Italy and around the world. At one point Nureyev was asked to stage his version of Cinderella for the San Carlo, and asked Angelini to dance the leading role. "The circle was closing," he said. "I went back to dance at the San Carlo as an invited principal dancer and, as I promised so many years earlier, I did charge them a fortune."

Angelini had some work in the new world as well, with Ivan Nagy in Cincinnati and at Les Grands Ballet Canadiens de Montréal, and liked it well enough that when he heard Tulsa Ballet was looking for an artistic director, he decided to apply, never thinking he would be offered a directorship. Twenty-five years later, he is very proud of what he has accomplished in Tulsa:

> I came here to a company with a $1.5 million budget, three studios, maybe $7 million in assets and endowments, no international or major national touring experience, short contracts for our dancers and no school. Today, our organization has two buildings, a school (started in 2002), a total of ten studios, two theaters and $40 million in assets and endowments. Our repertory is second to none. Our dancers enjoy the fifth largest contract in the country.

Dances created in Tulsa have been performed by European companies, including the Deutsche Oper am Rhein in Dusseldorf and Turkish State Opera and Ballet, and in Asian companies such as the Universal Ballet in South Korea.

Since taking over the reins of Tulsa Ballet, Angelini has never applied to another company. "This is my home," he said. Initially, he missed the applause that he was so used to receiving when he was performing, but he soon realized that he shared the applause with his dancers every time they took the stage. "We share the process of preparing the work and we share the pains that it takes to create excellence," he said. About ten years ago, he did return to the stage to perform Madge in La Sylphide. "But that didn't do it for me. Now, I belong in the audience," he said.

Angelini reflected on the special challenges that the ageing process presents to dancers:

> As dancers, we are used to watching ourselves with minimal clothing, six or seven hours a day. The problem is when you stop dancing, the only way to keep the same body is to keep working out six or seven hours a day. We all know that is unrealistic and downright impossible. As we grow older, we need to be smart about how we push ourselves. Trying to do what we did when we were young is not just downright stupid, it is dangerous. And yet, we need to push against our limits and maybe just a tad beyond them. It is, after all, the constant thrust toward the extension of our limitations, both physical and mental, that keeps us going. The only difference between 25 and 50 is where the wall that defines your limits really is.

Angelini exercises seven days a week, arriving at work at 7:00 every morning. First, he answers emails and then does a class by himself. It is the same class he will give the company later that day. He does it in a half hour to make it aerobic. But when teaching, he limits his movements "for a couple of reasons," he said. "First, dancers tend to unconsciously imitate the person in front of them, and I don't want them to acquire my mannerisms or shortcomings," he said. And second, "we get cold and it's easy to rip something, especially at our age," he said.

When asked what he looks for in a student today, he said, "Someone with excellent training, great versatility, decent physical talent, and a love and commitment to dance and to the company." His definition of artistry: "The ability to go to far-off places with our minds and hearts and even more importantly, the ability to take people around you to that magical site. It can be shaped but cannot be taught—definitely not easy to come by."

He still thinks of himself primarily as a dancer. "In the back of my mind, yes, once a dancer, always a dancer; it's just that now my energy is directed in a different path," he said.

His advice to any student considering going into the profession:

> Unless you love dance to the point where you need to dance—not necessarily that you like to dance but that you need to dance—don't go into the profession. Just do it for fun. The world is changing and the economics of dance are shifting. The repertory of most companies has widened in scope and in artistic, technical and stylistic range. We all have fewer dancers and

expect them to dance everything well. Fewer jobs, more qualifications, short careers, and not a lot of money—dancing is not a lifestyle. It is definitely a vocation.

Candace Itow

Firmly Grounded

Can you dance with a herniated disk? Can you dance until age 54? You can if you're Candace Itow. Now in her mid-60s, (she looks 45) Itow said she probably would have continued to dance longer if she had not been offered the job as director of membership with AGMA (American Guild of Musical Artists), where she heads a department of five people overseeing contracts and collecting member dues. Itow started in a volunteer position with the union before getting her paid position ten years ago.

Itow is another case of where "everything just sort of happened." She had been dancing ever since she could remember. Her father was a TV repairman who listened to music all the time, and Itow remembers dancing in the living room whenever the music came on. At age seven she put on performances for her parents (she was an only child) and would even serve refreshments (tea and Coca-Cola) to her captive audience, dressed in "lots of petticoats — in those days people wore petticoats," she said.

Around that time, an aunt took her to see her first ballet, the Ballet Russe at the Academy of Music in Philadelphia. "It was about a unicorn and I was so excited, that's all I remember." She began lessons with the Philadelphia Civic Ballet Company at age nine. There was a performing company attached to the school, and by age 13, she was given solo roles, performing in communities around the city. She was thrilled to get paid but didn't think about making a career of it.

At age 17, she came to New York to study at the American Ballet Theatre School with Madame Perejaslavic. "Madame Perejaslavic made you very strong," she said. "She had come from the Ukraine where she had danced and had taught for The Royal Ballet in England—many of the principals, including Fonteyn and Nureyev, went to her when they were in New York." At age 19, Itow was invited to dance with the Pittsburgh Ballet Theatre, after Nicolas Petrov noticed her in class. She was dancing solo roles, yet still didn't think of ballet as a career. "I was just so absorbed in it, but I do remember thinking I would rather do this than anything else in the world," she said.

In 1970, Perejaslavic recommended her to Thomas Andrew, director of the New York City Opera ballet, and when a spot opened in 1971, she joined the company that was to become her dance home for the rest of her career. She never auditioned. "It was clearly a case of being in the right place at the right time—they just took me," she said. There were only eight dancers in the company and she danced group numbers in operas such as *Faust, Rigoletto, The Merry Widow, La Traviata, Julius Caesar*, along with being a soloist in *Mefistofele*.

Just as planning a dance career was not a conscious choice on her part, neither was transitioning out of ballet. Over the years she had taken classes to explore the fields of physical therapy, computer programming, and massage therapy, but nothing took. At the opera she became very involved with labor negotiations as a volunteer union representative, "not just for the dancers, but for the singers, dancers, musicians — I ended up doing it for everybody," she said. She found she was good at it, also drawing from experience gained in her side job with an attorney.

By age 54, although she had stayed in shape, it was becoming harder to dance. She had been suffering from a herniated disc since her late 20s. "I was told to quit when I was 30, but I couldn't," she said. "I hung in for another 24 years." Although her back was always painful, she had learned to manage it with a lot of physical therapy and not much medication. When budget shortfalls at NYCO led to dancers being given fewer and fewer performance opportunities, Itow knew it was time to quit.

"I did miss performing," she said, "but not the applause — I missed the people I worked with." As she reflected on her unplanned-for career, Itow said it had all worked out for the best. She realizes she probably would not have lasted with a ballet company, with its grueling schedule and the greater demands placed on dancers' bodies by a more challenging rep. At NYCO Itow had only had to dance a few nights a week, and even that limited schedule had tailed off over the years, extending her career. "There was less and less for us to do, no more *Merry Widow,* no more splits, but I probably still could have done a split [at 54]" she said, laughing. "I'm not so flexible now," she said, "but I get up at 8 a.m. and work till 7 p.m. every day. If I could find the time to study yoga, I think I would be as flexible."

Bruce Wells
In It For The Long Haul

He had a body that wanted to dance. That's the way Bruce Wells, faculty member of Pacific Northwest Ballet School and former New York City Ballet principal, described his initial introduction to ballet. Wells, who grew up in Tacoma, Washington, recalled, "I skated first at about age seven or eight. The best ice skaters studied ballet and I had a friend who wanted to study so I went with him." Up to then, Wells' only acquaintance with ballet had been watching a performance by The Royal Ballet on TV. When he saw the class, Wells had an epiphany. "I saw this girl, Noel Mason—to this day we're friends," he said. "She was doing run, run, grand jeté and I knew from that moment that was what I wanted to do."

Wells began lessons at age nine. "I studied with a wonderful teacher, Patricia Carino. She was British—if my teacher had not been British, my mother would not have had the confidence in my studying ballet in America. At the time, the feeling was Americans knew nothing about ballet. I received scholarships right away. Thank God," said Wells.

Wells studied one or two days a week which grew to every day by the time he was 12, remaining with Carino to the age of 15. In the summer, he went to the The Banff School of Fine Arts in Canada, where he said he also had some wonderful teachers.

In 1962, he saw NYCB at the Seattle World's Fair. He also saw the Bolshoi Ballet, The Joffrey Ballet and The Royal Ballet. "The Bolshoi was doing a ballet called *Ballet School* by Asaf Messerer. They used about 15 students locally. I auditioned and they hired me," he said. Wells remembered seeing American Ballet Theatre when he was 11 at a local theater in Tacoma. "It was George Balanchine's *Theme* and *Variations* and *Les Patineurs* and Toni Lander in *Miss Julie*, and I said, 'This is it — I have to be on that stage.'"

In 1965, Balanchine sent the ballerina, Jillana, to Tacoma to scout for talent. After seeing Wells dance, she invited him to come to the School of American Ballet summer course financed by the Ford Foundation. At the end of the summer, he was one of 25 students the director, Diana Adams, chose to remain and study during the winter. This was the prelude to Wells being asked to join the company in 1966. He was promoted about four years later to soloist.

While signs pointed to the fact that he would be a principal dancer one day, Wells began to look at the experience of those around him after they no longer danced. "I thought, 'What am I going to do?'" he said. Wells had choreographed a workshop piece which Balanchine critiqued. "That started me thinking this was what I wanted to do with my life. I was only 20." He did not see choreography as a career transition. He saw it as the next career step.

He choreographed a piece to Tchaikovsky for six girls from the local ballet school in Tacoma, then returned to NYCB. The piece attracted notice. "Doris Hering wanted to codify everybody in the nation through the National Association for Regional Ballet (NARB)," Wells said. "She created seminars for participants in various schools who would get together and perform for each other." Wells' ballet was chosen to be part of one of the festivals.

Wells credits his first teacher, Patricia Carino, for planting the idea in his mind as a youngster that there were many ways you could be part of the dance world:

> She opened us up to all the possibilities of dance when I was just a young boy—not just the ballet. On Saturdays, she would roll out rolls of shelving paper and we'd be on our knees on the floor hunching over these pieces of paper. She would say, "Design a tutu for a ballet that you're going to choreograph, and now design the scenery." She sowed the seeds for me to become a choreographer before I realized it.

Wells struggled with ankle and knee issues from stress and strain and by age 31 had spent a lot of time in physical therapy to maintain his instrument. Once he decided not to perform in his 30s, he started to heal. He noticed that now that his body was becoming "human" again.

Wells described his conflicting thoughts and emotions at the end of his performing career:

> I had to mourn the loss of that time in my life. On the other hand, what I was moving into was demanding in a very different way. My career became more scholarly. You're constantly investigating new ideas musically—Mozart, Tchaikovsky, Mendelssohn. You're generally out of the studio. You're moving away from the domination of your physicality and you're freer to explore other areas.

At 6 feet tall and 160 pounds, Wells remains in remarkably good shape. "I still lift girls," he said, "and I do sit-ups and push-ups." He tries to walk to the studio every day if he does not go to the gym. The musculature of his body has been slow to change. He strongly advocates listening to your body. "I don't jump very much," he said and added laughing, "I'm in a culture of youth, so if they don't see me jump around, they're not missing very much."

He narrates and performs character roles in children's ballets five or six times a year. "At this age (mid-60s), I'm wearing wigs and beards and there's a lot of acting," he said. His roles include two original characters in children's fairy tale ballets: the Father in *Snow White* and the Sandman in *Hansel and Gretel*, who protects the children while they're sleeping.

When asked if he missed the kind of applause and adulation he received as a performer, he said, "No, because as a teacher, I have it every day." Like so many other ballet teachers, his dance studio has become his stage. "You go into a room and everybody is focused on you, everybody bows. When you leave the room, everybody applauds."

Victoria Beller-Smith

Confronting Terpsichore

Victoria Beller-Smith wants to clear something up: "If you find you're in pain, stop dancing!" As a young girl she'd read Agnes de Mille's book, *Dance to the Piper*. "The gist of it was it is noble to suffer for your art. I romanticized what she said. I was very sensitive and impressionable and I took it to heart," she said. For several years, Beller-Smith ignored what her body was telling her and danced with an extraordinarily painful knee, which remained undiagnosed. This eventually ended her dance career at 25.

Beller-Smith comes from a theatrical family. At age 8, she saw *Oklahoma!* thirteen times while she spent a week with her grandfather, who was the press agent for the road company. Her aunt was the famous Spanish dancer, Carola Goya, who taught Beller-Smith how to do pliés and tendus when she was four. Beller-Smith would practice five minutes a day. "I didn't know what I was doing," she said. She started ballet lessons at Ballet Arts School in Carnegie Hall with Vladimir Dokoudovsky and his wife Nina Stroganova. Beller-Smith remembers watching the professional classes and being awed by the dancers, many of whom were members of Ballet Theatre. At age 13, she saw the Grand Ballet du Marquis de Cuevas in a New York performance and decided that was the company she would join one day.

Just before her 21st birthday, she was asked to join the Marquis de Cuevas Ballet as a member of the corps. "I was ecstatic. It was what I wanted more than anything else in the world. The principal dancers were Rosella Hightower, Nicholas Polajenko and Vladimir Skouratoff." It was not quite as glamorous, however, as she'd imagined:

> We worked year-round, with two weeks unpaid vacation. We were not protected by a union and would sometimes dance a couple weeks straight without a day off. We travelled mostly by train but sometimes by bus, plane or ship and we were responsible for finding our own lodgings—not an easy thing to do at midnight or 2 a.m. in a strange city.

Worse than the grueling schedule was the constant pain in Beller-Smith's knee. She thought if she were with a company that had a home base and did less touring, she could work harder and feel better. She read in Dance Magazine that the American Festival Ballet was going to be the resident company in Salzburg, Austria and wrote requesting an audition. One of the dancers, who had been with de Cuevas before Beller-Smith, recommended she be hired sight unseen. Beller-Smith flew to Europe but the company soon closed down, with plans to reform in a few months. By the time they did, Beller-Smith knew she could no longer dance. "I figured I'd better stop while I was ahead," she said, "if being ahead can be defined as being in pain most of the time."

Photography had been a hobby she shared with her father, and her parents agreed to foot the bill for six months of classes at the New York Institute of Photography. "I was perhaps naïve about my job qualifications—I applied for a photo assistant and darkroom job and was chased around a locked studio."

She tried an employment agency where she was told she had no skills. "I thought that entrechat six was a skill, but they meant typing and shorthand." She was nonetheless hired as a receptionist at a television studio, and after six months showed her portfolio to the staff photographer. "He said, 'I'm leaving, do you want the job?'" She soon discovered she could work in another profession besides ballet and find success and satisfaction.

She ended up marrying one of the copy writers, Harmon Smith, and as they planned to have a baby, she left the agency after four years to freelance, finding work doing photos for grade school textbooks, and projects for Lincoln Center and The Juilliard School. A collection of her personal work is housed in the New York Historical Society. When she was asked to take on an assignment using digital equipment, she decided to get out of the business. Today, all her work is digital and she is delighted with the possibilities.

But Terpsichore has always breathed in her heart. As she aged, she worked out once in a while with a former modern dancer who gave classes to older adults. "I did not tell her I had been a dancer," she said. "It was not ballet. We moved in a dancerly fashion appropriate to our age. One day, she took me aside and said, 'You must have been a dancer somewhere,' And I said, 'Yes' and I stayed in the class." She attends as many performances as she can, occasionally going on ballet "binges." She watches New York City Ballet and American Ballet Theatre on YouTube. "The dancers are extraordinary," she said.

"I still love ballet and I wish I could have continued it for many years," she said. "But I know I was wise to make the change while I was still young. I made a new identity for myself as a photographer, but ballet was always the greatest joy for me." To this day, people still tell her she looks like a dancer, walks like a dancer, or sits like a dancer. She smiles and says, "That's a compliment!"

ABOVE: Gemze de Lappe
Photographer: Marcia Rudy

LEFT: Robert Maiorano, 11 years old, Brighton Beach, Brooklyn, N.Y.
From the archives of Robert Maiorano

LEFT: Robert Maiorano as the Prince and Deborah Paine as Clara in a New York City Ballet production of *The Nutcracker*
Photographer: Martha Swope

RIGHT: Robert Maiorano teaching, Glens Falls Ballet Center
Photographer: Amy Ross

LEFT: Marilyn K. Miller
Photographer: Marcia Rudy

BELOW: Ann Reinking
Taken from DVD: *In My Hands: A Story of Marfan Syndrome*
Sister Productions, 9 Somers Place, Sag Harbor, NY 11963
A film by Ann Reinking, Brenda Siemer Scheider, Emma Joan Morris, DVD distributed by Film Makers Library, 124 East 40th Street, NY, NY 10016

ABOVE: Ann Reinking
Taken from DVD: *In My Hands: A Story of Marfan Syndrome.* Sister Productions, 9 Somers Place, Sag Harbor, NY 11963
A film by Ann Reinking, Brenda Siemer Scheider, Emma Joan Morris, DVD distributed by Film Makers Library, 124 East 40th Street, NY, NY 10016

BELOW: Juliet Seignious; Photographer: Marcia Rudy

LEFT: Violette Verdy.
New York City Ballet production
of *Swan Lake*, choreography by
George Balanchine (New York)
1969. ©NYPL

RIGHT: Raven Wilkinson
(teaching).
Photographer: Marcia Rudy

126 DANCE ON

RIGHT: Raven Wilkinson (teaching, far right).
Photographer: Marcia Rudy

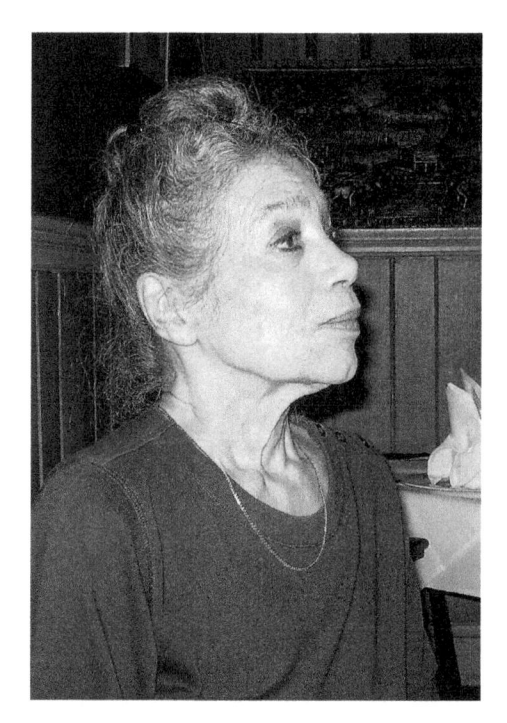

LEFT: Raven Wilkinson
Photographer: Marcia Rudy

ABOVE & BELOW: Marcello Angelini teaching class at Tulsa Ballet
Photographer: Ryan Allen.

RIGHT: Oleg Briansky
Photo by
Carl Van Vechten
From the archives of
Oleg Briansky

BELOW: Oleg Briansky
Photographer:
Marcia Rudy

LEFT: Carol Bryan
From the archives of Carol Bryan

BELOW: Gail Crisa
New York City Ballet, studio photo of Gelsey Kirkland, Gail Crisa, an unidentified dancer and Polly Shelton in costume for *Brahms-Schoenberg Quartet*, choreography by George Balanchine 1968. ©NYPL
Photographer: Martha Swope

RIGHT: Gail Crisa
Photographer:
Aaron Kesselman

LEFT: David Fernandez;
From the archives of
David Fernandez

Gail Crisa

Her Own Particular Rhythm

"It all began at age ten months," said Gail Crisa, sitting across the table of a West Side diner. "I stood on my toes in my playpen—I was always able to stand on my toes." Soon she started tap lessons, supplemented by acrobatics because she was so limber. At eight she enrolled at the Arcaro Dance Studio in Pelham, New York, run by four sisters, cousins of the jockey Eddie Arcaro.

One day, Crisa saw a student in the corner of the studio executing a ballet pose. She remembers thinking, "I need to do that." It was time to put on those pretty pink pointe shoes. "Then I saw *The Red Shoes*, and that was it," she said. At age 12, her mother took her to an audition at the High School of Performing Arts in Manhattan, where she entered as a freshman at 13. "That's where my real ballet training began," said Crisa. She was the dance award winner for ballet in her graduating class at age 16. She still has the trophy.

After graduation, Thalia Mara, one of the teachers at PA, invited Crisa to join her dance company, but Crisa's dream was to dance with New York City Ballet. It was well known that George Balanchine always chose his dancers from the School of American Ballet, so with help from a rich uncle she paid the three or four hundred dollars to take the summer course, after which she was given a scholarship.

At SAB she was put in a special class for a select group of advanced students, hand-picked by Balanchine and taught by Felia Doubrovska. Her fellow students included Susan Pilarre and Paul Mejia. Crisa was made an apprentice that winter season, and became a member of the company the following spring. "I didn't have a real plan, I just wanted to be a Balanchine dancer," she said.

She reflected on her early days with NYCB: "I think most girls hope they'll get married and raise a family. But it was different then. You didn't want Mr. B to know you had a boyfriend. We all wanted to please him." She recalled late-night steak dinners with friends and fellow company members Edward Bigelow and Suzanne Farrell, in the company of Balanchine. "He loved steak houses," she said. Crisa was always famished after a performance that might include four ballets, but remembers taking care to leave food on her plate, conscious of Balanchine's watchful eye. "He liked his dancers thin," she said. "When I was a young dancer, we thought that by not eating during the day, we would have the optimum thinness for the evening's performance," she said. "The theory has since changed. Dancers need to eat just to make up for the hundreds of extra calories they expend in energy each day."

Of the relationship between Balanchine and her close friend Farrell, she said, "It was never anything romantic. Suzanne was a very young girl. She was very flattered by all his attention and admired him, but I believe her love for him was more as a father figure."

NYCB was a 24/7 existence with Balanchine and, at some point, Crisa knew she wanted a 9-to-5 existence. She had never made the jump to soloist, and after 16 years in the corps she was ready for "a normal life":

The life of a NYCB dancer is anything but normal. You dance Tuesday through Sunday, every night. After 16 years in the corps—and I loved every minute of it—there comes a point where you're not getting the little solos or any new ballets to dance. How many years can you do *Stars and Stripes*?

She took a year off, to start to look around. The first job she applied for was advertised as a showroom manager. Instead, she found herself at the front desk as a receptionist. "All these men came from all over the country, typical salesmen, to buy their products, and like typical men they would hit on me," she said. "I was the first thing they saw when they came in. And I had good legs," she said, laughing. "That job didn't last long."

Crisa started looking again, and found a job with a real estate agency in New York City that is famous in the ballet world for renting apartments to dancers. "When I was interviewed, they asked what I had been doing. I said I was a dancer. They asked, 'Where did you dance?' and I said, 'New York City Ballet.' And the interviewer said, 'You're hired!'—he loved ballet." The job grew into an office manager's position, where Crisa remains today.

"I still miss performing—you never get over it," she said. "Nothing in my life has ever taken the place of dancing, and that's why I'm still doing it with kids half my age at Reebok Sports Club." It took Crisa a couple years after leaving NYCB to find a regular exercise routine. In addition to the gym dance class, which she attends two or three times a week, Crisa lifts weights and does Pilates. "It's very important to keep the core strong," she said, "but there is nothing like ballet—everything is elongated." Every once in a while her teacher gives a moving step, and the old thrill is there:

> You start in one corner of the room and you end up in the other, and it's very musical—there's something euphoric about it, I feel it in my entire body. I am thankful for each day that I wake up and can still take a dance class—no matter what else I do, I will always be a dancer. It will always be in my soul.

Rose-Marie Menes

Ballet and Beyond

"Many people feel that when you step outside of New York City, you cannot find proper ballet training," said former Ballet Russe de Monte Carlo soloist Rose-Marie Menes. But as artistic director of the Westchester Ballet Center for the Performing Arts, in Yorktown Heights, she has worked to change that perception.

"I never really wanted a school," she said. As a teacher for many years she had seen the demands placed on her directors and decided it wasn't for her. But her partner, Denis Selvo, wanted to work at a school. Menes agreed to help, and after two years, when Selvo left, she was left to run the school, raise her daughter, teach master classes and perform.

She recalled the moment, at age five, when she knew she wanted to be a dancer. The Sadler's Wells Ballet had come to Miami, and her mother had bought tickets:

> We arrived late. The first ballet was *Swan Lake*. As we searched for our seats in the dark theater, I looked up at the stage and saw the swans all lined up and that was it. I just knew at that very moment that is what I wanted to do with

the rest of my life. I was mesmerized—my mother had to keep pulling on me to sit down.

Menes started taking ballet classes at age six from local teachers in her hometown of Hialeah (a small residential suburb of Miami), but her father, conditioned to think that Russians made the best teachers, scoured the phone book until finding the name Georges Milenoff in Coral Gables. "It was the best thing he ever did for me," added Menes.

No one in the family had ever danced. Her private lessons with Milenoff were a loving sacrifice for Menes' mother, who took a job in a Miami sweatshop to pay for them. Little did Menes know that being exposed to her mother's sewing at a very young age would pay career dividends many years down the road.

Menes went from Milenoff to Mme. Maria Swoboda, head of the Ballet Russe School in New York City, where she was offered a scholarship. At 17, she joined the American Festival Ballet, and at 18, the corps at the Radio City Music Hall Ballet, where she was promoted to soloist and danced for two and a half years. In 1965, Menes auditioned and was accepted by Ballet Russe de Monte Carlo.

But Ballet Russe had its limitations. For one thing, the company only performed certain months of the year. "I was not earning a living from dance," Menes said flatly. As for job security, the company went bankrupt three years later and Menes found herself laid off at age 23.

But a teaching career began to take shape. She was offered a position by Thomas Andrew at Ballet Brio, began working with Eugene Tanner in the state-funded Title 3 program, and taught at Carnegie Hall. She also worked on the ballet workshop circuit for ten years, mostly with Art Stone's Dance Olympus and Dance Caravan, where she was performer, teacher and choreographer. "I soaked everything up like a sponge for ten years," she said. After the first week of tour, she was asked to be a principal dancer. Menes designed her own tutu and began to work with Blasia Amacio, the head of the costume department. "I never asked for the job, I just added another hat," she said.

"I knew there were other things I wanted to do besides dancing," Menes explained. While with Ballet Russe, Menes had taken the trouble to find out how every single tutu was made, preparing for the time when she would no longer dance. "If I've learned one thing in my life, it's that if someone asks you to do something, never say 'I'll think about it.' Always say 'Yes.'"

At age 37, Menes completed her transition away from performing. When she speaks of her stage career, the word "love" is what shines through:

> I danced because I loved dancing. I didn't dance for the applause. I loved dancing the second act pas de deux of *Swan Lake*, but I also loved being in the corps. I loved taking dance classes and rehearsals and being part of that whole fantastic dance world. If I had never become a principal, I would still have loved it."

Her love for teaching is also evident. "I'm like a mother to these kids." she said. "They tell me things they would never tell anybody else." She continued, "That is the way I felt about Georges Milenoff, my first teacher in Florida. He was my friend. He opened my eyes to a world outside of dance. My goal in teaching has always been to get them to love dance as much as I have." Menes takes her students to New York to attend ballet performances at American Ballet Theatre, to expose them to the story ballets. "I wanted the boys to see the fencing sequences in *Romeo and Juliet*, to see how "macho" ballet could be, that dancing did not make them sissies. They loved it."

Menes has had her share of injuries, including one hip replacement and two knee surgeries. Ironically, the hip replacement came not as a result of dance, but because of a fitness trainer's failure to understand the dancer's body. "He told me to turn my feet in when going down in a squat. After all those years of training with the hip turned out at the socket, when you force it in the other direction, you are grinding the bone," she said. After one of her knee surgeries, a therapist again told her to exercise with her foot turned in. But this time she explained that her foot needed to be turned out. After a week, her flexibility was almost normal.

In the last few years, as a concession to age, Menes has stopped much of her demonstrating, relying on her advanced students to show the more technically challenging combinations. I can't do piqué turns or pliés, but I can still point my feet," she said, lifting a leg to reveal an exquisitely-pointed, high-arched foot. Menes described her goals for the future:

> I want to train students well enough so that if they want a dance career, they will be able to join

New York City Ballet or ABT. But I tell my kids, "There's a big world out there, and you never know where anything is going to lead you." At age 69, I still don't know where I'm going to go.

140 DANCE ON

David Fernandez

From the Field to the Playground

David Fernandez is known as a dancer's choreographer. "I don't come in to impose my ideas," he said. "My first job as a choreographer is to win over the dancers. If I do that, we have a chance of succeeding in our endeavor." He allows dancers to review the structure of the dance, and together they share creative energy. "I always want to make the dancers look good," he added.

Fernandez has been teaching for more than 25 years and choreographing for almost that many, mostly as a contemporary ballet choreographer. But he came late to dance. Growing up in Mexico, he was always the quarterback on school football teams, until about age 15. "I was too short," he said. He got into a boy band, but was cut just when they got a record deal. His cousin, a tai chi master, arranged for Fernandez to meet Tita Ortega, a ballet teacher whose studio is affiliated with the Royal Academy of Dancing. "I was 17—too late by most standards for a professional career," he said, "but Tita gave me a test for flexibility and physicality and afterward said I could be in her class."

He was placed in the lowest level, with eight- and nine-year-old girls, and given some free private lessons. "Most men were offered free lessons in Mexico," he said. "They still are, in fact all around the world it's the norm." Fernandez worked his way up to the advanced class in four and a half years, but began to realize he would never be a professional dancer. He didn't have enough technique or a great body for dancing. "By the time a company scout sees you at 17, you should already be dancing on a performance level," he said.

He did find work though, in commercials and on a tour to Puerto Vallarta doing breakdancing and jazz. "I said, 'Wow, I'm getting paid for dancing,'" he recalled. At 21, he met a woman who saw him as a choreographer, and forever changed his path. He began to study the choreographers whose works he had danced at Ortega's school, and Ortega invited him to choreograph and dance a section of one of her dance.

Fernandez described the evolution of his choreography, and a fairly-recent breakthrough:

> At first I was really choreographing as a test for myself, I wanted to show that I could choreograph so I worked really fast. Then I realized things didn't look finished. About six years ago, I hit a wall. I wasn't going anywhere. I would choreograph whenever someone would call. Finally, I met someone who opened my eyes. She saw my work and helped me to realize my strongest point is my musicality but I wasn't using it.

Fernandez described his method of choreographing by drawing on the paper tablecloth at the restaurant where we spoke:

> I call the preparation my playground. Here is the swing, here is the slide, then I go and play unrestricted. I may not have any idea of what I'm doing, but I know how many counts I need, and how the solo will fit into the overall piece—it could be a solo, duet, or trio. Every choreographer has his own way of notation—there is no right or wrong way as long as it works.

Inspiration may come in the studio, in a dream, or from listening to the music for the next piece as he travels to the next job. Or from the dancers. Fernandez loves his dancers. "They come into my mind when I think of a piece." Fernandez likes to have at least three weeks advance notice, but doesn't always get that luxury:

> I can choreograph in crazy time if I have to. Joaquin De Luz (pricipal dancer for NYCB) needed a solo recently. He called me on a Monday and said he needed it in five days to go to Russia for "Kings of the Dance." I got it done. Last year, Sacramento Ballet called me for a piece four months in advance. That was easy.

Now most of his commissions call a year in advance, which gives him plenty of time to create. He has done annual work for CelloPointe, a ballet company in New York City, which he says has been a dream place to play out his musicality:

> This has been a jewel for me. They use live music. I have choreographed from Hayden and Mozart

and I could choreograph from Beethoven to Pink Floyd to AC/DC.

Fernandez recently turned 50 but says age has only brought increased self-confidence. "I remember thinking, 'Now that I'm 50, I know what I'm talking about,'" he said. "It's weird because I have this energy, this vitality, my ideas make more sense to me, they come faster and clearer."

An avid collector of rejection letters, Fernandez says if a dancer isn't getting rejected they're not doing their job. "Sometimes you get rejected, sometimes you think you were bad, but you get hired—it's all in the game," he said. "Not everyone can be a principal dancer," he said, "but that doesn't define your career. I'm so glad that things worked out the way they did."

Donna Silva

At One with the Music

As a child, Donna Silva experienced music as dance. She recalled visiting the Tanglewood Music Center in Massachusetts as a youngster at camp:

> We were on a day trip and had picnicked with thousands of other people on the grounds. When the concert started and the conductor lifted his baton—it was either George Szell or Leonard Bernstein — people rushed to their seats. But I didn't. I began to walk around the grounds, dancing in my mind, and I was transported to a time when I was taken to ballet and music concerts. Sitting in my seat at a music concert, I would imagine dancers coming out on stage and taking their places, especially if the music was Stravinsky, Mozart or Tchaikovsky. Sometimes I invented choreography. I used to think there was something wrong with me, as everybody else seemed to be satisfied just listening to the music.

It makes perfect sense then, that after a long performance career, Silva would become Professor of Dance at the Boston Conservatory of Music.

"I remember dancing before I could walk," said Silva, who grew up in Fairlawn, New Jersey. She was put in ballet lessons starting at four. At seven her mother, who had seen a recital by Ballet Russe de Monte Carlo, took her to study with Lila Crabtree, a retired dancer from that company. When Silva was 12, Crabtree told Silva's mother, "I've taught her all I know," so she was enrolled at the American Ballet Theatre School. From ABT, Silva went to the Metropolitan Opera Ballet School where she studied with Margaret Craske, Antony Tudor and Alfredo Corvino and was handpicked by Alexandra Danilova and Igor Youskevitch to perform in several opera ballets.

She was chosen as an apprentice with The Joffrey Ballet in 1965. While apprenticing, Lucia Chase asked her to join ABT, but Silva signed a contract with Joffrey the following year, where she stayed for seven years. "Joffrey was very interested in the youth, and I was getting more acting roles," she said. At 28, she joined the First Chamber Dance Company, directed by Charles Bennett, which was a group of ten principals from major dance companies. "It was a huge transition," she said. "I was growing up in every way. I learned a great deal there and carried that energy and drive, a sense of striving for perfection, throughout my career." Bennett choreographed, along with José Limón and Anna Sokolow, and the dancers rotated between soloist parts and dancing in the corps. The company toured extensively throughout the United States, and the dancers taught wherever they had a residency at a college.

For Silva, performing was never about the audience, it was the music. "I wanted to see if I could train my body to be at one with the music," she said. "Every time I went on stage, I would give thanks to be in the position of being able to dance and express the music."

Although Silva originally had no aspirations to teach, the teaching residencies were having an effect. "The more I taught, the better I got," she said. "If you want to teach students how to do a rond de jambe, you have to execute the technique, but they must never lose sight of the music and the passion. To become the music is the most beautiful experience ever," she said.

In 1979, the company folded. To keep her head above water, Silva taught at Cornish College of the Arts in Seattle and worked as a ballet mistress, but at 34, she still needed to dance. She went to Europe to teach at the Lucerne Theater, in Switzerland. "I wanted to dance so badly I just went and joined the corps," she said, which led to joining the Bern State Ballet and getting back into solo roles. Silva only stopped dancing en pointe when she was 40:

> The knees went. It was all connected to the lower back. I didn't know where to go to get physical therapy. There was no one to guide me. It killed me to have to stop. It took me ten years. I danced my last ballet and cried inside throughout the whole performance. I didn't want to stop but my body was just hurting all over.

In 1993, she came home and started over. She appeared in character roles with the Boston Ballet in 1994 and that same year joined the faculty of the Boston Conservatory, where she taught and choreographed for 22 years, receiving the Most Outstanding Faculty award four times.

Through a combination of Pilates, floor barres, mat work, and resistance training, Silva has managed to keep her body within just ten pounds of her performing weight:

> I'm lucky. I have people who help me take care of my body: nutritionists, acupuncturists, and a muscular therapist. It's important to stay toned. Walking is helpful and it's better to keep the power in your legs if you're going to teach. My problem is my knees. I don't turn or jump anymore. If I don't keep up with a stretching routine every day, I'm in agony.

She misses the applause and the chance to work closely with a choreographer, but has found fulfillment teaching. "As a teacher you can pass so much along," she said, "and I continue to dance from the inside."

William Whitener

Giving Back

After seventeen years as artistic director of Kansas City Ballet, William Whitener moved back to New York to explore what he viewed as the third phase of a long and productive career as performer, director, and now choreographer and teacher.

No one in his family danced. "We had singers and naturally-gifted musicians who played by ear," he said. Whitener traced the moment that he knew he wanted to be a dancer all the way back to age seven, as a boy watching dance on TV:

> I watched all the dance programs on television: Fred Astaire, the Ed Sullivan Show, the Arthur Godfrey Show, the Imogene Coca Show, the Jackie Gleason Show, anything I could dance along with. I was impressed with the way they moved. I wanted to be like them.

He began ballet training with Karen Irvin at the Cornish College of the Arts in Seattle. "It suddenly dawned on me that they were making a living as performers." He described his family as "flabbergasted" when he told them that he wanted to make a career out of ballet. "I guess we all knew it was going to happen by the time I was 15, because I had met Robert Joffrey and he had expressed an interest in my talent," he said.

Joffrey had brought his entire company to Seattle in the 1960s for a residency and created a summer school in Tacoma, where Whitener spent two summers during high school. In his senior year Joffrey asked him to come to New York as soon as he graduated, on a scholarship and with the promise of a job at New York City Opera Ballet, where Joffrey was guest choreographer. Whitener moved to New York in 1969, subsequently becoming a member of The Joffrey Ballet and dancing principal roles for the next eight years. The repertory incorporated jazz, ballet, and works by Jerome Robbins and Twyla Tharp.

In 1978, Whitener made the jump to the Great White Way, in Bob Fosse's *Dancin'*. Because of his jazz experience, it was not a hard transition for him, but he had to learn quickly because he was brought in to replace an injured dancer two weeks before the show opened in Boston. He learned all seven male roles as a dance alternate, then became first alternate when the show opened on Broadway. Whitener performed in New York for three months, before joining Twyla Tharp Dance.

At some point he noticed the height of his jump was beginning to diminish, and he saw it as a sign that he would need to find other ways of moving. He worked with Martha Clarke (one of the founders of Pilobolus) in a touring company of *The Garden of Earthly Delights*, which he described as "a group of mature dancers who no longer did the jumps—when we were flying, we were rigged up to an apparatus. It was a different way of moving."

The end of his performing days and beginning of his teaching days came in *Jerome Robbins' Broadway*. Robbins taught his works to Whitener, who then taught them to the other dancers. He described working with Robbins as "a unique situation."

Together they were retrieving very memorable moments from Broadway shows. "I realized we were doing something very special," said Whitener.

By that point Whitener felt he had accomplished most of his goals as a performer:

> My career occurred during a period when dancing had a high level of exposure. Joffrey had two seasons a year at City Center and there were international tours. There was Twyla Tharp. There was Broadway, TV, and film. I felt I had experienced a very fortunate time and I was ready to make the transition to artistic director. I listened to my body as I always did. At 38, I thought it was wise to stop professional dancing so I could exit in one piece and avoid complications from overuse.

Whitener attributes his career longevity to teachers and coaches who kept a close eye on him, Karen Irwin and Joffrey in particular, and to keeping a dialogue going with his body. That dialogue continues today:

> I'm in good shape with the exception of a rotator cuff—it was a tear that happened over time. I know I need to build strength around my injury, and having danced so many years, I know when to leave well enough alone and rest it. I'm getting control of it through therapy and treatment. I'm trying not to have surgery.

Today, to keep in shape he takes Pilates classes, swims at the YMCA, does gym exercises, and walks "tremendous distances" every day. "Of course as we age, everybody's body changes," he said. "I have to use my time wisely and select exercises that build strength and flexibility without overtaxing the body. I'm more careful now."

He plans to remain active in the theater world, and doubts he will ever stop. And he'll continue teaching. "I enjoy it so much," said Whitener. "There's a great satisfaction in giving back." He believes one key of good teaching is understanding that each student is unique. "Progress is made by treating people as individuals," he said. "There has to be a level of agreement in the class that there are common goals, but you can reach those goals without sacrificing your individuality."

He says the best advice he ever got was from Bob Fosse: "Dance till you drop."

Laura Young
Progressing Naturally

"Ballet and I grew up together," said Laura Young, one of the longest-tenured principal dancers in the history of the Boston Ballet (1960-89) and a current teacher there and at Dean College in Franklin, Mass. "I don't think it was a conscious decision I ever made, it was just a natural progression."

Young grew up in Cohasset, Mass. on the South Shore of Boston, in an artistic family. Her father was in vaudeville and studied violin with the concertmaster of the Boston Symphony Orchestra until he took off the tip of his finger in an accident with a saw. "But oh, could he ballroom dance," said Young. Her father's sister sang with a big band and her paternal grandmother played piano for the silent movies. Young's mother studied ballet until she was 18 and knew how difficult a life in dance could be, but never deterred her daughter from pursuing a career.

Young began ballet lessons at age six and loved it from the start. "My mother took me to see *Swan Lake* with Nina Novak when I was seven, and I was enthralled, never dreaming that one day I would dance it opposite Rudolf Nureyev," said Young. But it was Novak's offstage persona that made the biggest impact:

She was so gracious to a little girl who wanted her autograph desperately but didn't have a pen, using her lipstick to give me my heart's desire. She truly was a queen in my eyes — one to emulate.

At age 12, Young's teacher, Cecile Baker, sent her to study at the Boston School of Ballet with E. Virginia Williams and Sydney Leonard, who was Miss Baker's cousin. "Miss Leonard would often dance in our recitals as a guest, and her presence inspired me to work harder and emulate her finesse," said Young. At 13, she was accepted into the New England Civic Ballet, the company affiliated with the school at that time. They became a professional company when she was 16, and at 18, Young was made a principal dancer. At one point Young went to New York to study with Balanchine, who told her if she studied with him for a year he would put her into his company, but her parents were against the idea of her staying in New York alone.

Early in her career, Young performed in Brigadoon in 1965 on a three-tent circuit, and *Milk and Honey* with Molly Picon on a four-tent circuit, and says dancing in the round taught her a lot about stagecraft. In addition to her storied career with Boston Ballet, Young also danced with the Metropolitan Opera Ballet from 1971-73.

At about age 30, Young started guest teaching, knowing she would need to transition one day. She staged *The Nutcracker* for Georgia Deane, director of a local school, which has been performed every year for the past 27 years. She frequently taught at Walnut Hill School for the Arts for Sydelle Gomberg, who would later become head of the Boston Ballet School and recruit Young to teach there. But Young mostly credits Bruce Marks for mentoring her as a coach and choreographer, and giving her the opportunity to truly put her talents to the test by directing Boston Ballet II (where she choreographed seven ballets) and the summer dance program, all while still dancing. "I even drove the van," she said of that busy time.

Other influences on Young's dancing and teaching include "superheroes" Margot Fonteyn, Galina Ulanova and Alicia Alonso. She singles out Fonteyn for her purity and exquisite line. "I had the honor of dancing the Nocturne in *Les Sylphides* opposite her when she was a guest artist with the company. She did some insightful coaching for what we were dancing together, but just watching her in rehearsals was a lesson in itself." Boston Ballet founder E. Virginia Williams and the myriad of choreographers and guest artists she brought in were also hugely influential. "Each one had something to teach us," said Young.

Asked how she felt when she finally made the transition to full-time teaching, Young replied, "Elated that I had made it through *Don Quixote*—I was very injured." She says she was "ready to stop putting myself on the line." But Young maintains teaching is also an acting profession, in which she draws on theatrical skills to engage students in the classroom.

Despite the many positions she has held, Young refuses to be bogged down in titles. "I am a teacher," she said, modestly. "I coach if I am asked. I can craft a piece of choreography, but it's not something I am driven to do. I prefer to stage small ballets, but can do full lengths."

Like many dancers whose careers extended into mid-life, Young has dealt with her share of long-term injuries. She has had one hip replaced, several ankle and knee surgeries, and while she is not as flexible as she once was, she is strong. The hip replacement gave Young her life back (she had been walking very slowly, with a cane). Her exercise routine is now limited to a lot of walking. When teaching she tries not to ever leave the floor, but sometimes "it just happens," and she says she finds herself in the air, with a bubble over her head that says, "You idiot!" She would demonstrate full-out during her dance years, but now says she indicates, and leaves the rest up to her students. "Age speaks for itself," she says, and demands modification, accommodation. She is patient, resolute, and forward-looking. "I will see where the next natural progression takes me," she said.

Nina Novak

Nothing Is Difficult

That graceful and gracious ballerina who captured the heart of Laura Young as a child, with her performance but mostly with an autograph signed in lipstick—where does such a fabulous creature come from? In Nina Novak's case, from war-ravaged Poland and the horrors of Hitler's camps.

Novak's artistry was discovered when she was in the first grade in Warsaw, Poland by a folkloric gymnastics teacher who insisted that Novak's parents take her to the National Ballet School. After being admitted to the school along with her brother Edmund, nothing else interested Novak. "I never thought of selecting another career," she said.

She had distinguished teachers, including Bronislava Nijinska and Leon Woizikovsky. During World War II, ballet lessons with Woizikovsky became a sporadic affair for five years, interspersed with dodging war planes. At times, there was no place to have a class—she would arrive at the studio and discover it had been bombed. But she continued to study wherever she could.

Things took a darker turn during and after the Warsaw Uprising. Novak was forced to hide in a cellar as her house was bombed. Her father died in Dachau and a brother in Auschwitz. Novak was ultimately sent to a labor camp. After the camp was liberated in 1944, she was reunited with her mother in Wieliczka.

After the war, Novak visited America with the Polish National Ballet and was spotted in a performance at the New York World's Fair by Sergei Denham, who offered her a contract to join the Ballet Russe de Monte Carlo in New York as a member of the corps. She quickly rose to the rank of first soloist, then prima ballerina. One of her most memorable roles was that of the lead can-can girl in Gaîté Parisienne. She also danced in *The Nutcracker, Coppelia,* and *Le Beau Danube.* While performing with Ballet Russe, she taught in the Ballet Russe School in New York City under the title Maître de Ballet.

In 1964, she relocated to Caracas, Venezuela, founded a company and opened a school, the Academia De Ballet Clásico Venezolano, where she remained for over 50 years and was looked upon as an icon. But political turmoil haunted both dawn and dusk of her distinguished career. For years, the government of Venezuela has suffered widespread corruption which in recent years led to the collapse of the economy, widespread malnutrition, and an alarming crime rate, forcing Novak to flee for Philadelphia, Pennsylvania where she continued as teacher and private coach. "I am staying in Philadelphia until Venezuela is free," she said.

While Novak has not performed for many years, she still feels a deep connection with the audience to this day. "I have always loved the audience," she said, "and I have been very lucky to have always been accepted by it." At the end of each performance in Caracas she took the stage to share the applause with her dancers.

"Classical ballet is the most difficult profession for a woman," she said, "as the body has to remain in perfect condition physically." She attributes her long career to proper nutrition, and being wise in selecting different roles as she aged, based on her physical abilities. She has stayed in good physical condition and says this is critical "if you are active as a maestro-choreographer or director." Novak identified "early marriage, children and family life," as challenges in the life of a ballerina. "Classical ballet awakens one's sensibilities as well as one's artistic qualities," she said. "When we live with passion for the sublime art of classical ballet, nothing is difficult."

Amos Chalif (1918-2012)

Between Two Worlds

Amos Chalif always lived in multiple worlds. Like many working-class young men of his generation, he was a Boy Scout and would go off to fight in World War II. But he was also a dancer.

We sometimes forget, when we talk of the Greatest Generation, of their valor and their can-do attitude, that among the returning soldiers were gentle souls, poets and painters, even dancers. Amos Chalif was such a man. Returning from the U.S. Army Air Corps (the predecessor to the U.S. Air Force), he sought to mold the world through movement and dance until his death at age 94.

Chalif was born and raised in a five-story building at 163 West 57th Street in Manhattan. The apartment served as both dance studio and home for the Chalif family for decades. His father, Louis Chalif, who emigrated from Ukraine in 1902, was called "the first Russian ballet master" to come to the U.S. In addition to ballet, the studio offered ballroom, tap, pantomime, and even fencing, attracting many students from among the elites, including Rockefellers and Carnegies. It was also the first dance school in this country to offer teaching degrees in dance. "Before that, anybody could hang up a shingle," Chalif said. "People from all over the world came to study and take the two-year course we offered." There was a final exam which included all types of dancing, with oral, written, and demonstration components. The staff of 14 included Leon Varkas, the teacher of Cyd Charisse (who used to come to the studio to study ballet).

An unusually flexible and talented student, Amos Chalif began performing in his father's annual recitals at age nine, and in the then-legendary dance concerts at Jones Beach. At one point he performed at the Waldorf Astoria Hotel for Franklin Roosevelt's birthday.

Chalif tells an interesting story of the time he and other Boy Scouts attended an international jamboree in prewar Europe. The group stayed at a castle in the Rhineland, and were escorted through several airplane and glider factories. After the tour, the boys were invited to sit down for a treat of hot chocolate with "a nice little man" named Adolf Hitler. "We didn't know any better," Chalif recalled. "All we knew was that we were traveling and we went wherever the itinerary took us. At age 15, we had no sense of what was to come."

Chalif enlisted in the Air Corps before Pearl Harbor. "I wanted to see if I could do something else besides dance," he said. He was assigned to a bombardier squad whose mission it was to bomb Germany. "I thought it would be fitting to revisit Hitler by dropping bombs over Germany," said Chalif. Chalif received his overseas orders in April of 1944, married his fiancée two days later, then flew supplies over the Himalayas to China for the remainder of the war. He never got his chance to revisit Hitler.

After the peace, Chalif completed 14 years of active duty followed by two decades of intermittent duty in the Reserves, rising to the rank of Colonel. He divided time between his Air Force administrative duties, some of it at the Pentagon, and teaching dance in Chatham Township in New Jersey, where the Chalifs settled and opened the first of several schools where he taught ballet along with ballroom.

"At age 67, I was still demonstrating everything: grand jetés, and entrechats deux," he said. "Two were enough." He taught adult classes, which included many senior citizens. "I lifted all the female seniors," he said, "and never dropped a one." His students loved him because he did not take dance that seriously, and they always felt comfortable in his class.

One amusing distinction in a distinguished life: when noted illustrator Tim Hildebrandt was hired by Parker Bros. to paint portraits of the suspects in a special edition of the popular board game Clue, he turned to Chalif to be the model for Colonel Mustard. "He knew I was a colonel in the military," said Chalif, "and ironically my family had been in the mustard business at one time."

Chalif remained in excellent shape through his 80s, even though he never worked out. He attributed his excellent condition to good genes and good food (mostly fruits and vegetables). It was only after he decided to retire in 2005, at age 87, that everything started to go downhill physically. "It was the biggest mistake of my life," he said. "I should have kept right on teaching."

Daniel Duell

Still Prepared to Deliver

In 1968, while watching New York City Ballet perform at its summer residence in Saratoga Springs, 16 year-old Daniel Duell had an epiphany: "This is what it can be. This is where one can go," he remembered thinking. Edward Villella in *Rubies* and *Tarantella*; Violette Verdy in *Emeralds, Firebird*, and *Swan Lake;* Peter Martins and Suzanne Farrell in *Diamonds;* John Clifford in *The Nutcracker;* little did he know he would soon be joining them on stage.

Duell, who is now in his mid-60s, began studying ballet at age 11. His father, who had taken some modern dance classes while in college, and his mother, an elementary school teacher, were completely supportive of his decision to make ballet a profession, which came at age 14, when he performed the title role in Josephine Schwarz's *Amahl and the Night Visitors* for the Dayton Civic Ballet:

> What took hold inside me at the time was the exhilarating experience of being part of a community cohered around the precise, polished delivery of ephemeral moments of truth to a large group of people we all largely didn't know. There was also the magic of the beautiful story, its wonderful Gian Carlo Menotti mu-

sic and Miss Jo's insightful and engaging choreography. Without saying it to myself, I felt like this could be a very nice way to spend a life.

Duell credits his early teachers in Dayton, Josephine and Hermene Schwarz, with pointing students toward career possibilities. They invited Balanchine to visit the Dayton Civic Ballet in 1963, which was followed by annual visits from Violette Verdy, the "scout" for NYCB. Duell was accepted into the School of American Ballet in the summer-fall of 1969, where his teachers included Stanley Williams, André Eglevsky, Alexandra Danilova and Suki Schorer.

"I did come up through the ranks," he said. Duell spent three years at SAB before joining NYCB, then five years as a corps member, two as a soloist, and eight as a principal. NYCB was the first and last professional company he joined. And what a place it was. His dance idols included Jacques d'Amboise, Villella, and Martins, along with Verdy, Patricia McBride, Gelsey Kirkland. Williams and Jerome Robbins were his greatest teaching influences. He also credits d'Amboise with having taught him "worlds about partnering."

Duell's favorite ballets and roles from that era include Balanchine's *Brahms-Schoenberg Quartet*, the first pas de trois of *Agon*, Franz in *Coppelia*, the boy in green in Robbins' *Dances at a Gathering*, the spring section of *The Four Seasons* and the man in purple in *The Goldberg Variations*.

One day Mr. B approached him in company class and told him to learn everything about technique—the fine articulations of pointe work, how a ballerina dances, how a male dancer dances, and the importance of making male dancing just as clean and specific as a ballerina en pointe. "He told me,

'One day you're going to teach,'" said Duell. That turned out to be prophetically true.

Duell's performing career was temporarily interrupted when he suffered a lower back injury that resulted in a ten-month hiatus from NYCB. In some ways the injury extended his career, as his rehabilitation and recovery process included weight training, which improved the safety and efficiency of his partnering for the rest of his life. By the fall of 1980, Duell returned to the company in full form.

In 1987, Duell was offered the artistic directorship of the Chicago City Ballet, leading to his retirement from performing in September, 1988, dancing Balanchine's *Tarantella*. After hanging up his ballet slippers he did miss getting out there as a dancer, "prepared to deliver," but Duell always felt he would remain a part of the ballet world. "I had the flute as backup," he said, having begun classical training at an early age (Duell once accompanied soloist Sherry Moray in a CCB production of his ballet *Ave Maria*). Duell has managed to remain in front of an audience, one way or another, as emcee, lecturer, demonstrator and educator.

Recent projects have included teaching and

coaching at the Royal Danish Ballet, participating in Balanchine Masterworks at the Harris Theater for Music and Dance with Ballet Chicago, setting ballets for other companies as a Balanchine Trust repetiteur, and a full slate of teaching, directing and choreographing at Ballet Chicago. He draws energy for all this by getting plenty of exercise demonstrating in class and practicing gyrotonics. In other ways, "you have to simply accept inabilities due to ageing," he said.

He hopes to one day play the flute for performances again, to write a book about his life in dance, and to continue enjoying life after dance with wife Patricia. He tells his dancers to make the most of their training: "The lessons learned are exceptional tools for any direction you may take in life, and there are many options for a non-dance career. But there is only one window of opportunity for developing as a dancer."

Darla Hoover

Twice Blessed

"I always wanted to dance," said Darla Hoover, Associate Artistic Director of Ballet Academy East's graded children's program in New York and Associate Artistic Director of the renowned Central Pennsylvania Youth Ballet. At the same time, Hoover, who danced with New York City Ballet for eleven years, was always preparing for the day she would no longer dance. Today, she is one of the most respected and sought-after children's ballet teachers in the world.

Hoover began ballet lessons at age six in Carlisle, Pennsylvania with the celebrated Marcia Dale Weary, who founded CPYB in 1955. She received early exposure to world-class performances thanks to a dedicated father, who drove his daughter to Washington, D.C. whenever American Ballet Theatre would visit. She also remembers summer intensives at ABT in New York City and also Philadelphia where Weary took select groups of students for a week at a time. "In those days you could go to open classes. Kids took class every day we were there." Weary had students performing from age six on, and somewhere along the way, Hoover decided she wanted to become a dancer.

Hoover moved to New York at age 15 to study at the School of American Ballet, still in the Juilliard Building at that time, while attending the Professional Children's School. After two years, she was taken in as an apprentice. "Once a year, usually in October, Balanchine would come to class and pick out apprentices. At that time, union rules were that an apprentice could dance *The Nutcracker* and two other ballets."

At age 17, she was made a member of the corps without being told. "One of the ballet mistresses came up to me and said, 'Did you sign your contract?' and I was so shocked, I said, 'No,' and she said, 'Well, you've been taken into the company.'" The ballets of Balanchine hold a special place: "When you dance Balanchine, it feels as though you are dancing many different ballets because the ballets have such great range," she said. *Serenade* stands out as a favorite. "It's a masterpiece, a marriage of Tchaikovsky's music and Balanchine's choreography," she said.

During her performing career, Hoover was able to return frequently to Carlisle, where Weary would always let her teach, enabling her to gain a foothold in teaching while still dancing. When the time came for Hoover to make a career transition, she says she never felt the angst or sense of loss many dancers experience. It felt more like a continuation of what she was doing.

The transition came with a fracture of her left shin that forced Hoover to leave NYCB at age 29. "It started as a stress fracture, but I kept dancing until it developed into a regular fracture," said Hoover. While the fracture was healing, Hoover became pregnant and was a stay-at-home mom for two years.

Then came a call from Weary, who had gotten permission to do *The Nutcracker* at CPYB and wanted Hoover to dance it. She did, and never returned to NYCB. Peter Martins asked Hoover to take a leave of absence, but she decided to keep freelancing instead. Blessed with a very flexible body, Hoover hadn't lost any flexibility during her two years off. "I transitioned at a time when I danced full-out," she explained. Hoover continued to perform until age 57.

Hoover is committed to a strenuous physical routine, which includes working out in the gym two hours a day, stretching, doing one hour on a cardio-treadmill or elliptical machine, and lifting seven or eight-pound weights for her upper body. She remains in great shape, but not what she refers to as "dancer shape." She laughed, "I'm old so my body has changed, things are looser than they used to be." She doesn't kick as high as she used to, but she can still do a backbend, and she can still jump because her legs are strong from all the cardio.

Hoover teaches about 200 students, 15 classes a week, including a pre-professional children's class for ages 7–19. In addition to the demands of two world-class programs in two different states, Hoover is an in-demand repetiteur for the George Balanchine Trust. Sometimes, while demonstrating, she finds herself dancing more full-out than she anticipated. "I never lost the sense of how wonderful it is," she said. But teaching and helping her students find careers in the dance world is what fills this master educator's soul:

> Dancing is very self-centered. You have to take care of yourself, you think about yourself all the time. It's much more gratifying to take care of others. You get to do that as a teacher.

Bruce Marks

Looking Back – Looking Forward

"I have achieved more than I could have dreamed of," said Bruce Marks, former American Ballet Theatre principal dancer, former artistic director of Ballet West and the Boston Ballet, and current Chairman of the International Jury at the USA International Ballet Competition.

Now in his late 70s, Marks said he never planned for such a long and productive career. He grew up in New York City and decided to become a dancer at age 13, the first in his family to excel in dance or any art form. He studied at the High School of Performing Arts, where his teachers included Antony Tudor, Margaret Craske, and Pearl Lang. It was Tudor who suggested he join the Metropolitan Opera Ballet, which he did in 1956, being promoted to premier danseur in 1958. Then in 1961, Tudor suggested Marks join ABT, where he was promoted to principal dancer shortly after his arrival, the youngest in the company.

During his fruitful career with ABT, Marks created one of the male roles in the American premiere of Harold Lander's *Études*, as well as the leading role of Prince Siegfried in ABT's first full-length version of *Swan Lake*. He excelled equally in ballet and modern dance, also dancing in ABT's production of José Limón's *The Moor's*

Pavane, becoming the first man outside Limón's company to dance Limón's roles.

Marks remained with ABT for ten years, making guest appearances with the Royal Swedish Ballet and the London Festival Ballet, and marrying ballerina Toni Lander in 1966. In 1971 he became the first American principal dancer with the Royal Danish Ballet, where he stayed for five years, mastering the work of August Bournonville and appearing in Paul Taylor's *Aureole*.

Marks ended his onstage career in close to top form, though eventually he needed double hip replacement. Today he keeps himself in shape with regular gym workouts and water aerobics. When asked if he missed the audience's applause he said no, because as a teacher, he has it every day. "You go into a room and everybody is focused on you. Later, everybody bows and then applauds you when you leave the room."

For his second act, Marks became co-artistic director of Ballet West at the invitation of Willam Christensen and following Christensen's retirement in 1978, assumed the title of Artistic Director. From 1985 to 1998 he directed the Boston Ballet, transforming that company into the world-class institution it is today. In his directorships, Marks always sought to foster the work of young choreographers, and he is recognized as a pioneer in innovative dance education and outreach programs, most notably by creating Boston Ballet's Center for Dance Education City Dance, a tuition-free ballet training program for urban public school students. In 1998 he created Arts Venture, Inc., a dance consulting firm dedicated to passing along the vast knowledge and insight he accumulated over his long career. Said Marks, "I plan to spend my last years transferring the information I have to anyone who wishes it."

Peter Naumann
Slippers Trump Sneakers

Peter Naumann says he dances in his sleep. "I point my feet. When you've done tendus all your life, you even do them in your sleep." After nine years of pre-professional training, a 26-year career with New York City Ballet, and 20 years as Artistic Director, Ballet Master and Resident Choreographer at New Paltz Ballet Theatre, that's understandable.

Naumann, who is in his 60s, started dancing at age three in his hometown of Babylon, N.Y. "I don't know if you could call it dancing—I went to some woman's home," he said. He began ballet studies at nine when his mother took him to the Eglevsky School of Ballet in Massapequa, N.Y. No one in his family danced. His father worked in an A&P supermarket warehouse but was always there to help when Eglevsky put on a show. His mother was a stay at home mom.

"I can't say I loved ballet from the beginning," Naumann said in a phone interview. "My love for it developed over a period of time," he explained, though a rare opportunity at age 13 must have helped that process. Naumann was approached by a woman who knew Princess Grace and needed a boy to accompany her girls to perform for the princess. He travelled to France where he studied for two weeks in Cannes prior to the performance, which was the prelude to a summer vacation in Switzerland.

The Eglevsky school sent him on to the School of American Ballet. For years, Naumann made the long daily commute into New York City from Long Island, studying part-time in school and taking correspondence courses. Luckily, SAB paid for everything including commuter expenses. When Naumann finished his studies at SAB, Balanchine invited him to join the company. "I remember thinking, 'Thank God! I can get out of the house and move to New York City,'" he said. With a paycheck and ballet career before him, he made the jump, never graduating high school. "I have to give my parents credit because they let me do it," he said.

Naumann's long career with NYCB spanned the years 1970-96. He remained a corps dancer but was given numerous solo roles from very early on, including *The Four Temperaments, Episodes and Dybbuk*. His favorite partners included Rene Estopinal, Wilhelmina Frankfurt and his future wife, Lisa Chalmers. His favorite ballets included Jewels, *Symphony in C and The Four Temperaments*. "Balanchine would give you the idea, but there seemed to be more freedom, allowing the dancers to explore the movement and letting them find themselves," he said.

Naumann was very happy at NYCB and never thought about a career transition:

> I didn't see the end was in sight or think I would one day lose my job. It was Peter Martins' decision. He told me I wasn't going to be rehired for the next season. It was a surprise to me. I had been working under Peter for about thirteen years, and I was still dancing between five and seven ballets a week. It was kind of a shock. 26 years is a lot of time.

After reaching that decision though, Naumann says Martins and NYCB were extremely generous and helpful. Still it was hard. "There is a period of time where you don't know who you are because you're not performing so much," he said. More than the applause and acceptance of the audience, Naumann missed the adrenaline rush of getting to dance the ballets. "Dancers have something to get up for every day," he said. "You have to give everything you've got, and the stage is the place where you can do it. It's a wonderful release." A dance career, he said, is "like trying to be in the Olympics for your whole life."

With a family to support, Naumann says he "didn't do a lot of sitting around thinking about what I wanted to do." He knew when he left NYCB he had to find work quickly, and he found it in New Paltz, with the New Paltz Ballet Theatre and a home studio he opened with his wife.

Naumann was fortunate to remain mostly injury free. At one point in his career he had some cartilage removed from his right knee, which he described as devastating because he was on crutches for three months:

It was a much bigger procedure in those days. They didn't have microsurgery. When I came back to NYCB, Balanchine said, "Don't do a grand plié. You don't need it." I never did a grand plié after that.

He says he is still in good shape—no back trouble, no hip replacements, and he can still jump. "Of course the body changes with age. I'm certainly not capable of doing what I did 30 years ago." He goes three times a week to the gym, and still demonstrates in class. "I would have to say doing ballet is still my favorite physical activity. Going to the gym is a little boring," he said. "Ballet is a set of exercises that achieve a certain goal. When you have done it your whole life, those exercises feel the best for you." Even in your sleep.

Lois Bewley (1934-2012)
Trailblazer

She danced before she walked, but never planned on becoming a dancer. As far as Lois Bewley was concerned, she always was one.

Destined for international stardom, Bewley grew up in a little town outside of Louisville, Kentucky, in an area she described as "real country." In one of the truly remarkable careers in early American ballet, Bewley would perform with the Ballet Russe de Monte Carlo, New York City Ballet, American Ballet Theatre, Jerome Robbins' Ballets: U.S.A., and on Broadway, as well as help found an internationally-praised chamber ballet group for which she was dancer, choreographer and costume designer. And she was funny. The New York Times dance critic Anna Kisselgoff called Bewley "one of dance's finest comediennes" and her infinitely-pretzled parody of the Balanchine style, *Pi R Squared*, was described by the Times as "brief but devastating."

At age four Bewley acted in her country school recitals, which she described as "really elaborate, with remarkable costumes made of crepe paper." She remembers playing Little Bo Peep in an antique dress from her grandmother's attic. She saw her first ballet in 1944, at age 10, when her mother took her to see Alicia Markova and Freddie Franklin. No one in her family danced but her father, who worked in state government, had a perfect dancer's body. "I'd say, 'Do first position,' and he would. I'd say, 'Do you know how many dancers would kill for your turn out?'" Her mother was a teacher and a painter, and both parents were very supportive of her dancing.

Ballet lessons began at 12, she was en pointe at 13, and in the professional class at 14. "I would be there before class started and practice after class," she said. At 16, she did summer stock then went to the School of American Ballet in New York, where she says she was miserable:

> I went because my teacher wanted me to. I studied with Muriel Stuart, who felt sure I could join New York City Ballet but thought I should wait six months because I wouldn't get the personal attention once I was in it. I really wasn't ready psychologically for the New York experience, and I became depressed, so I went back to Kentucky. I guess I was homesick.

Back in Kentucky, she did more summer stock, enrolled in college, and continued to dance, ending up in the Louisville Ballet. At one point Leon Danielian came to town to stage a ballet he was dancing with Ballet Russe, saw her, and advised her to come back to New York. Several months later she did.

Bewley danced with Ballet Russe for a year and a half. "I don't think I ever auditioned. I just took class and was invited to join the company." She also studied at the Ballet Theatre School, and the same thing happened again: "They just watched you and invited you to join—it was actually a good way to choose somebody," she said. She went on a summer tour with Ballet Theatre but felt frustrated dancing in the corps, having already done solo roles with Ballet Russe. Then Vida Brown, Ballet Mistress at New York City Ballet, asked her to join as a soloist.

A year later, Bewley and two other City Ballet dancers, William Carter and Charles Bennett, founded the First Chamber Dance Quartet, which she described as "a remarkable little company that originated the term 'chamber dance.'" They were subsequently joined by Nadine Revene and Janice Groman. First Chamber Dance Quartet debuted to acclaim at the 92nd St. Y in November, 1961. The tiny group of dancers toured the US and Canada in a station wagon attached to a trailer for four years. In 1965, they visited West Germany and Belgium and were an enormous success, which led to the U.S. State Department arranging a world tour in 1969. Between March and June, they visited twelve countries, including Indonesia, Greece and Thailand. The company dissolved nine years later because of personal differences between the founders.

In 1972, Bewley directed the American premiere of Carl Nielsen's comedic opera *Maskarade* for the St. Paul Opera, for which she also choreographed, designed the costumes and danced. "[Directing] is a natural talent I didn't even know I had," she said. Bewley would go on to a successful second career choreographing and teaching for ballet companies and operas around the country and around the world.

Along the way, Bewley underwent a hip replacement for osteoarthritis, which she attributed to how she was built. "The left hip didn't turn out as much as the right, but it still turns out plenty," she said. At the time of our interview, Bewley was still able to do a stretch in which she placed the unoperated right leg next to her ear. "When I was with NYCB, Balanchine loved it when I raised my leg up," she said.

There was a time when everyone in the dance world knew who Lois Bewley was. But memories fade, people age. "You have to be very visible to get the jobs," she said, "and I'm not," Today she focuses on her embroidery. Ever the dancer, and ever the creative force, Bewley says she has not given up hope of doing more choreography.

Colleen Neary
No Regrets

Colleen Neary was eight years old when she decided she wanted to dance. She remembers seeing a performance of *Medea* at New York City Ballet, and there were children on stage. "I told my mother I wanted to start ballet because I wanted to be on stage." Her mother replied, "Oh no, not another."

Neary's trail had already been blazed by her sister Patricia, ten years her senior, who would go on to become a principal dancer. Although the girls didn't come from a dance family per se, their mother had done some vaudeville and could tap and had basic ballet, while their father, who died when Neary was nine, had been an actor at one point.

Neary, who was brought up in New York, followed her older sister to the School of American Ballet, where her first teachers were Antonina Tumkovsky and Hélène Dudin. Her idols and mentors growing up included her older sister, along with Maya Plisetskaya and other Russian dancers of the 60's. She spent a few weeks as an apprentice with NYCB, was taken into the company as a member of the corps in 1969, when she was 16, was promoted to soloist and danced with the company until 1979.

"I loved to watch Melissa Hayden—she was a second mom to me," Neary said, "and Jacques d'Amboise, Peter Martins, Patricia McBride, and of course, first and foremost, Balanchine. I looked up to all the principals at NYCB in the 70's," she said. Neary also began teaching at that time, and was on faculty at SAB from 1975-79.

"I am unusual," Neary said, "because I transitioned twice in my life and career." She left NYCB to become ballet mistress for her sister, who had become director of the Zurich Ballet. Neary remained in good shape and two years later was coaxed back onto the stage by Nureyev, performing as a guest artist in Verona, Munich, and numerous galas throughout Europe.

The second phase of Neary's performance career continued with Maurice Bejart from 1984-86, whom she credits with helping her to find her dramatic side by letting her explore herself in the many roles he choreographed for her. Neary then joined the Pacific Northwest Ballet, where she was a principal dancer from 1986-92. She credits Kent Stowell and Francia Russell for giving her a second, flourishing career at PNB. "It was fantastic for me," she said.

Neary had married fellow PNB dancer Thordal Christensen, and at age 40, felt she wanted to scale back while she was still at the top of her game, and start a family. The couple joined the Royal Danish Ballet, Thordal as a soloist and Neary as both dancer and ballet mistress. She would continue dancing character roles for many years, and having given birth to two children, also took on the challenging role of mom.

Now in her 60's, Neary and Christensen currently serve as co-artistic directors of Los Angeles Ballet. The company started in 2004 and had their first performances in 2006. They then opened a school, where they have directed and taught since 2008. Neary teaches classes and "runs around a lot," which helps her stay in shape—her typical workday stretches from 9:00 a.m. till about 8:00 p.m.

Neary feels she made the right decision to scale back her dancing when she was still at a peak. She had been more fortunate than most, for, while she had her share of minor pulls and sprains, she avoided any major injuries. She also avoided the challenges of dealing with fading technique:

> The reality is that when you get older, you must realize that you cannot do what you did at 20 or 30, and that is a transition. Transitioning is a physical thing, but it is also a mental place. If you mentally love what you are transitioning into, then you should have no regrets.

These days Neary no longer thinks of herself as a dancer. "I am a teacher and a director and I was a dancer," she said. But she still has the motivation and discipline of a dancer. Her future plans include building and furthering the company and school and continuing to teach Balanchine ballets. She passes on to her students a bit of career advice from Balanchine, who told her to just dance and not analyze too much, to just love what she was doing. "He also lived by the philosophy of 'live for today and not tomorrow or the past,'" she said, "in other words, do what you are doing now to the fullest, which I always did."

Frank Ohman (1939-2019)

Serendipity

Frank Ohman started tapping when he was four, inspired by Gene Kelly in *Singin' in the Rain* and *An American in Paris*. "My mother took me to see these movie musicals. I told her I wanted to become a tap dancer just like Gene Kelly," recalled Ohman, founder, ballet master and artistic director of the Ohman School of Ballet in Commack, N.Y.

It was only after his mother pointed out that Kelly had studied ballet that Ohman agreed to take ballet lessons at age 12. Raised in San Bernardino, Ca., he began lessons with Vera Lynn and Charles Barker. His stepfather worked for the railroad, and the family moved around a lot. "My mother encouraged me, but she was a very practical person," said Ohman. "I finished school early, and she said, 'Frank what are you going to do—ballet or college?' I said I'd try ballet."

When he was 16 he went to visit his grandmother in Los Angeles and saw his first ballet at the Shrine Auditorium. He remembered seeing Ballet Theatre with Youskevitch and Alonso in the *Black Swan Pas de Deux*, John Kriza in *Billy the Kid* and *Fancy Free*. "I thought, 'Oh my God! Ballet is not all swans.' It was so athletic," he said. Then he saw *Seven Brides for Seven Broth-*

ers, with Mark Platt and Jacques d'Amboise, and Carousel, also with d'Amboise, all of which made a great impact on him. "I sat through it twice in one evening. I thought, 'What masculinity!' His leaps—such power! When I saw him in the dream sequence ballet, I told my mother if I could learn to dance half that good, that would be terrific."

Ohman studied with David Lichine, Roselle Frey and Ernest Belcher (Marge Champion's father), who encouraged him to go to the San Francisco Ballet School and study with Lew and Harold Christensen. It was an auspicious move. After nine months, Lew Christensen took him into the company. After three years in the corps he was promoted to soloist, even after taking six months off to serve in the U.S. Army Reserves.

While Ohman was in San Francisco, Diana Adams from the New York City Ballet came and watched his class for a week, and asked him if he would be interested in auditioning for Balanchine. In 1962, Ohman was welcomed into NYCB. In addition to being familiar with Balanchine's style, Ohman was a quick learner. "He didn't need boys. They had boys. I was an extra. But we were going to Russia and one of the boys in the company left. I got his parts. I danced in *Fanfare, La Sonnambula*, and *Symphony in C*," he said.

Ohman recalled those eventful days on the Russian tour, which coincided with the Cuban missile crisis:

> They were throwing stones at the American Embassy. We all ate in one dining room in the Hotel Ukraine and stayed together the whole time. We were like a family. We would get notices every day about what was happening. Although the situation was very frightening, the company was very much appreciated by the audiences. They loved us. Once, when I was walking alone near the hotel, some guy came up to me and wanted to buy my shoes—he needed shoes. Nobody had ever come up to me before

and asked to buy my shoes. I had to tell him, "No, these are the only shoes I've got."

Ohman spent 22 years as a soloist with NYCB, partnering some of the world's greatest ballerinas, including Allegra Kent, Maria Tallchief and Kay Mazzo. The company knew he was trying to start his own school. "But they were very good to me. They kept me anyway," he said.

His agent, Mel Howard, produced the New York Dance Theater for which Ohman proved to be a very fertile choreographer. He ultimately devised over 200 ballets, and had his works produced by the Boston Ballet, the Syracuse Ballet, the Cassandra Ballet of Toledo, the Edmonton Ballet in Canada, and the Long Island Lyric Opera, among others.

The transition from performing to directing, teaching, and choreographing never affected Ohman emotionally. He explained, "I had danced so much when I was young, I really got my fill of it physically. Other things come into your life. You get married and have children, you have responsibilities."

Ohman left NYCB in 1984, the year after Balanchine passed away. He had founded his school five years before. "There was no point in staying. I couldn't be in two places at the same time," he said. "I loved to perform and now I try to teach children to love it. They are like little sponges. I love to watch them get it." His students range in age from 7-18, but the school also allows many alumni to take classes and perform in shows. Ohman has presented The Nutcracker for over 30 years, in which fellow NYCB alumnus Robert Maiorano has often performed as Drosselmeyer.

Ohman says he has fallen in love with yoga and Pilates to stay in shape. He studies yoga once a week with Lana Russo in Kings Park, N.Y., and said he practices all the time. "I'm older, but my weight is the same," he said. He has never had any injuries, which he attributes to always being very careful and warming up for at least 15 minutes. Now in his mid-70s, Ohman can still execute a pirouette and rond de jambe in class. "I have an older student demonstrate the really hard things," he said."I just keep doing what I love. God has been good."

Hilda Morales
Making Her Mark

Hilda Morales' list of teachers and mentors reads like a "Who's Who" in the ballet world. "It would be impossible for me to mention everyone," she said. There were Ana Garcia, Gilda Navarra, and Juan Anduze at Ballets de San Juan, where she started dance studies in her native Puerto Rico at age eight. Then there were all the teachers at the School of American Ballet, including Balanchine, Muriel Stuart, Hélène Dudin, Antonina Tumkovsky, Felia Doubrovska, Alexandra Danilova, and Nicholas Magallanes (who recommended her for a Ford Foundation Scholarship to study at the school when she was 14).

In her professional career, Morales was mentored as a soloist at American Ballet Theatre by co-directors and founders, Lucia Chase and Oliver Smith, along with Dimitri Romanoff, Antony Tudor, Patricia Wilde, Enrique Martinez, and Agnes de Mille. At Pennsylvania Ballet, where she became a principal dancer, there were Barbara Weisberger, Ballet Master Robert Rodham, and Edward Caton. And at Colorado Ballet, there was Director William Thompson.

Morales was placed on solid footing by her teachers in Puerto Rico. Sisters Ana Garcia and Gilda Navarra were co-directors of Ballets de San Juan company and school, teaching ballet and flamenco respectively, joined by their cousin Juan Anduze, who also taught ballet. Garcia and Anduze had studied at SAB, and Garcia had danced for Balanchine both at New York City Ballet and its predecessor, Ballet Society, and with Ballet Nacional de Cuba. Navarra danced with Jose Greco's flamenco company and became well-known in Navarra, Spain (hence the name change). At age 12, after attending a performance by Ballet Russe de Monte Carlo of *Giselle* at the University of Puerto Rico, with Alicia Alonso and Igor Youskevitch, Morales knew she wanted to pursue dancing as a career.

She also knew that eventually all dancers must retire, and prepared for it early, starting teaching in her early 20s at the Central Pennsylvania Youth Ballet summer program in Carlisle, Pennsylvania. "When I was ready to retire, one stage of my life ended, and another took over," she said. "I truly enjoyed performing, and now I also truly enjoy teaching. They are totally different, and both are exciting and interesting. When she finally stopped performing, she was also looking forward to being a wife and mother.

Now, as assistant professor of dance at Hartt School of Dance at Hartford University, Morales teaches classical ballet, pointe technique, ballet pedagogy, and coaches students in ballet repertory. She feels it is her duty to pass along what she learned from her own all-star line-up of teachers. But the best advice she received and now passes along to young dancers came from her parents: "It's all about work, how to prepare yourself."

Morales marvels at today's skill levels, and the demands placed on young dancer's bodies:

> Dancing has become more athletic through the years: lots of quick, fast feet movements, high leg extensions, intricate high jumps, and very complex choreography. I work with students that do modern (Limón and Graham techniques) and do lots of falls to the floor, which tend to be hard on the body. In the Cuban school, they do not start the class with grand pliés because they find it is hard on the body.

She finds that starting the class with slow movements of the feet and legs (battement-tendus), lots of bends of the upper body and port de bras tends to warm up the body quickly. She places the grand-pliés after a series of slow battement-tendus exercises.

Morales has not performed in close to 40 years, but stays in shape through her love of walking and gardening. She had a hip replacement about fifteen years ago, but has learned to adjust to it. In the classroom, she demonstrates arm movements fully, but indicates the position of the legs with her hands and arms. She sometimes explains the dynamics and musicality of a step by singing the music, while marking the step. She is very emphatic on this point: "I am not in the studio to dance. I am in the studio to teach."

The first things she looks for in a student are an enthusiasm for the art form, and a love of learning. "I think it's a great formula," she said. As for artistry, she says, "You either have it or you don't." And for those who have it, artistry can be cultivated through broad exposure to a variety of different dancers and styles of dancing, as she herself had: "It takes many layers, and a deep understanding of the art form to become an artist," she said.

Delia Peters

From Bookworm to Ballerina

When asked if she always wanted to dance, Delia Peters flatly said, "No." Then she added laughing, "When I was a child, I wanted to stay home and watch cartoons on Saturday mornings." But she was small for her age, and the family was concerned enough to take her to a doctor, who said, "Let her study ballet—it will put muscles on her." Peters, who grew up in Queens, New York, tells the story of her inauspicious start: "My mother dragged me, screaming, to the local ballet school when I was about eight. My reward was going to the library after ballet class, because I loved to read."

Her family, following doctor's orders, remained committed to the ballet lessons, even if she wasn't, and at the year-end show her teacher told her mother, "Your daughter has talent. You have to take her into the city to study." There were only two schools to choose from at the time: the NYCB-affiliated School of American Ballet or Ballet Theatre's school. Peters' mother went to see performances of both companies and preferred Balanchine's choreography to the story ballets which Ballet Theatre specialized in.

Peters was enrolled at SAB. On her first day there was a mix-up and Peters was placed in a class with all teenagers:

> Of course I was the smallest one in the class, and Madam Tumkovsky told me to make eight grand battements — front, side, and back — so I did. Then she took me by the hand and went to the office and said, "Put her in Children's Division III."

Peters was advanced after one year, and given the opportunity to perform in *The Nutcracker*. "They put me in a costume and paid me $6 a performance, and I remember thinking that was what I was going to do when I grew up," she said. She ended up appearing in every *Nutcracker* until the year before she joined New York City Ballet.

Peters spent 20 years at NYCB dancing demi-soloist, solo and principal roles, and had featured roles in several Jerome Robbins ballets including *Fancy Free, The Concert*, and *Dances at a Gathering*.

But something of the bookworm, the little girl who loved the library, remained inside:

> The last three years I was dancing, I was also attending Fordham University because I hadn't finished Professional Children's School and never got a high school diploma. They said if I took certain courses at Fordham, they'd give me a high school diploma, so I did. The first course I took was on Dante's *The Divine Comedy*. It was very difficult but I loved it so much that I decided to go to college.

Three years into her college studies, Peters injured herself while on tour with NYCB in Paris. Suffering from extremely painful torn hamstrings that never really healed, she went right on soldiering through, victim to "dancer denial," until the morning she woke up to the realization she was working too hard, and it was time to stop. She didn't bother giving notice:

> Right before the ballet, I went up to Peter Martins, who was standing in the wings, and said, "Peter, this is my last ballet. I'm retiring after this." I had to run around to the other side of the stage to make my entrance. When I got there. I heard him yell, "What?!"

The day after the performance, Martins called her into his office. He had Jerry Robbins on the telephone. They both knew she had been attending Fordham and planned to go to law school, but they wanted her to stay with the company and asked her what she would like to do. Peters responded that she thought that there should be a NYCB archive and offered to help start one. Robbins, aware of her abilities as a photographer, said he would like her to videotape his rehearsals with his corrections for archival purposes.

Peters photographed Robbins' ballets for a year, and taught in the Saratoga summer program but realized it wasn't for her. "It was not something I wanted to do for life. If I couldn't perform, I didn't want to be involved in ballet on that level," she said.

Peters went on to attend Columbia Law School, but found herself shadowed by her past. At her first law firm position, she was frequently introduced as "the dancer," and often wrestled with her own core identity. "I was the associate lawyer, but in my heart I was still a dancer," she said. "I missed being a part of a group of people all working creatively toward that curtain going up at 8 o'clock. I missed the camaraderie, the unity of purpose," she said.

Peters reports her body hasn't really changed over the years because she has an excellent metabolism, never had a sweet tooth, and eats healthy all the time. Without adequate time to exercise she realized she had gained a little weight, and like so many other dancers who have transitioned, began Pilates. "Pilates is excellent, particularly as you get older. There is no age ceiling," she said. She also has a trainer. Fortunately, there have been no knee or hip surgeries. "My feet loved pointe shoes," she said.

Peters currently works as counsel to a boutique law firm, but has her own clients as well, some of whom are in the ballet world. She has done work for the Balanchine Trust and produced a video tape for them. She has also done a lot of free work for former dancers.

What does she miss most about NYCB? "Waltzing," she said, recalling *Vienna Waltzes* with partner Bruce Padgett. "That last section, when we all wore those incredible gowns—Balanchine taught us how to waltz." And the camaraderie. The NYCB dancers of her generation have remained close, getting together every year for the last twenty years. They remain a family. "You help each other any way you can," she said.

Lawrence Rhodes (1939-2019)

A Noble Instructor

In his mid-70s, Lawrence Rhodes, Artistic Director of The Juilliard School Dance Division, shows no signs of slowing down.

Rhodes describes himself as a "movie person" whose initial dreams were all about tap dancing. Growing up, it was all about Fred Astaire up there on the screen, where life always seemed to be so wonderful.

Rhodes was born in West Virginia and moved to Detroit when he was two years old. He remembers a girl he met in grade school, Glenda Ann Busch, a tap dancer who became his first dancing partner. They took class together at the Capital School of Music and Dance. Between the ages of 9 and 14, he performed locally as a tap dancer.

Rhodes was brought up on country and western music. His father played the mandolin and his mother sang country and western and also loved social dancing. He described her as being "tremendously supportive" of his dancing. "She saved her money and paid for my costumes. Then at 14, I saw *The Red Shoes* and I said 'What is that?'" It was around this same time that he saw Ballet Theatre perform *Swan Lake*, and Alicia Alonso and Igor Youskevitch in *Le Combat*. With apologies to Fred Astaire, he became enchanted by the world of ballet.

Rhodes studied at the Armand School of Theatrical Arts with Violette and David Armand once a week for three years. Then Ms. Armand told him he needed to increase his weekly lessons. In 1957, he left for New York, becoming a student at the Ballet Russe School, working days as a bookkeeper in Union Square to pay for his evening classes. At 18, he was invited to join Ballet Russe as a member of the corps. He began studying with Robert Joffrey and in 1960 became a principal dancer with The Joffrey Ballet. Joffrey was supported by Rebekah Harkness and in 1964, Rhodes became a principal with the Harkness Ballet, after Harkness and Joffrey parted ways. His fellow dancers subsequently chose him to become the artistic director, and he stayed in that role until the Harkness Ballet folded in 1970. Rhodes then moved to the Netherlands where he and his new bride, Danish ballerina Lone Isaksen, danced with the Dutch National Ballet in Amsterdam.

Rhodes returned to the U.S. the following year where his choreographic career took hold. His first major piece, *Four Essays*, was for The Joffrey Ballet Studio Company. Fate can work quickly in the ballet world. The co-director of the Milwaukee Ballet saw *Four Essays* and wanted to buy it. Rhodes went to Milwaukee to stage it, which eventually resulted in his becoming director of the company in 1978.

At age 38, although he was still dancing well and in good shape, Rhodes was ready to begin a transition to teacher and choreographer, after 22 years of performing. He had watched two of his favorite dancers, Eric Bruhn and Rudolf Nureyev age on stage, and that convinced him to retire while he was still on top of his game. "All of a sudden, they were not jumping as high," he said. Rhodes reflected on the effects of retirement on his body and his sense of identity:

> I'm certainly bigger than when I was dancing, and it's reasonable to assume technique changes with age. I think it happens gradually in both directions. First you get better and better, then slowly things begin to dissipate. Everybody is different. But today people are dancing longer. I felt that I had had a very long and fruitful career with only minor injuries.

Rhodes spent a decade at New York University, first on the dance faculty, then as chair of the dance department, then another decade as the artistic director of Les Grands Ballet Canadiens de Montréal, before taking over the reins at The Juilliard School's dance division.

At Juilliard he is responsible for everything, including choosing the dancers and overseeing the educational curriculum. With so much on his plate, his teaching is limited to about five hours a week, which includes two advanced classes. To listen to Rhodes speak, one senses teaching remains at the heart of what he does. "Teaching is about problem solving," he said. "For example, finding a way to help someone to achieve something they haven't yet achieved—it could be as simple as having to do with the placement of the foot or the way they hold the barre."

When auditioning students, he looks first and foremost for those who have a passion for dancing. "I look for how deeply involved they are in working, and the way they focus and concentrate. There is a lot to look for including the general physical condition, good proportions, a sense of gravity, and musicality, which can't be taught." He prides himself on the extensive communication between students and faculty. "If a student is in trouble, we talk to them. We say, 'What's going on? What do you imagine for the future?' We do not dismiss students easily."

In class, with Rhodes demonstrating, barre work is generally about 40 minutes. He continued, "The barre is about balance, control, music and coordination." He said he is a "back-man." "Dancing is all about connecting through coordination stemming from the back," he said. Rhodes said he does not miss the applause of audiences. "The students applaud after each class. I think it's wonderful."

Michael Vernon

Determined, Passionate and Obsessed

"I find teaching as satisfying as dancing," said Michael Vernon, Artistic Advisor to the Ballet School of Stamford and Professor of Music (Ballet) and Chair of the Department of Ballet at Indiana University. "But not at first," he added quickly in a phone interview. "Teaching requires a certain maturity. When you teach, you always teach from your previous experience. It takes time to develop your own voice as a teacher. Your teaching is a product of your own life, not just ballet life, your entire life's experience."

Vernon, who is in his 50s, started dancing at age 14 but wanted to be a performer since he was 12. Growing up in London, he originally wanted to be an actor, but soon discovered how difficult it would be. "I came to realize I would not be an actor. I was very practical," said Vernon.

Instead he found he gravitated to ballet. He has vivid memories of seeing his first ballet when his mother took him to Covent Garden to see The Royal Ballet's *Birthday Offering* by Frederick Ashton. Margot Fonteyn was dancing. Vernon described it as "love at first sight."

"No one in the family danced," he said, "But I was determined, obsessed, and passionate." He credits the Israeli au pair the family had as he was growing up with encouraging his early interest in ballet. "She said, 'Michael, you love it so much, you should take lessons.'" He began to study with Nesta Brooking, a local teacher, who worked with Ninette de Valois. Two years later, he transferred to The Royal Ballet School, where he studied with Léonide Massine and de Valois, who took a liking to him. "By the time I was 18, I wanted to do choreography. I was like an apprentice," he said.

Vernon was in all the student productions, including *Swan Lake* and *Romeo and Juliet*, and eventually made it on to the stage at The Royal Opera House at Covent Garden, performing in ballets with some of the greats, including Nureyev and Ashton. "There was no question about whether I would stay in the dance world once I started," he said. "I've always made a living from dance alone, and never strayed from it."

As the recipient of a travel fellowship from the Winston Churchill Memorial Trust, he was able to come to America for three months. Upon returning to London, he joined the London Festival Ballet, directed by Beryl Grey, who recognized his talent as a choreographer and made him a member of the choreographers' workshop. "Beryl maintained that you have to teach if you want to choreograph, and she got me a job at a very exclusive school in the countryside outside London," said Vernon. He was the first student to choreograph for The Royal Ballet and has choreographed throughout the world over the past 30 years, including for regional and repertory theater productions of *The Boy Friend, Kiss Me, Kate*, The Who's *Tommy*, and *My Fair Lady*. A career highlight was his solo for Cynthia Harvey in American Ballet Theatre's production of *'S Wonderful*, which was performed for President and Mrs. Reagan, and shown on CBS television.

Every master teacher has their own favorite teacher, someone who inspired and brought them along, and for Vernon it was Stanley Williams:

> Stanley was extraordinary; he was like a mentor to me—his musicality, his manner—but his examples were constructed in such a way that you had to intuitively understand him. The dancer learned by the construction of the exercises, and these gave you technique once you mastered them.

Vernon's tutelage with Williams began after Vernon joined the Eglevsky Ballet, based in Long Island, as resident choreographer and ballet master in 1976 (he was artistic director from 1989-95). Vernon recalled observing Williams teach at the School of American Ballet:

> He wouldn't let me take his class. He told me that once I taught and gave up performing, I couldn't take class. I was Ballet Master at the Eglevsky Ballet Company, and he didn't think it was appropriate. But I used to watch him and I learned so much anyway. I still use some of his principles in my teaching, for example, the principle of working one leg against the other.

Vernon's varied career has included teaching at Steps on Broadway in New York City, regular work for the Manhattan Dance Project, as well as choreographing for the ballet company and ballet school at the Chautauqua Institution. He has had a long association with Ballet Hawaii, Dance Theatre of Harlem, and the Alvin Ailey American Dance Theater.

Vernon has felt the body changes that come with ageing, but also the ones that have come with a change of locale. "In New York I ran everywhere. Now, since I've been at Indiana University, it's more difficult to do."

After many years of teaching, he remains nostalgic about the applause and adulation he generated from the audience as a performer. "But without sounding arrogant," said Vernon, "my students have become my audience." They hug him at the end of the class. He enjoys a varied schedule, and at Indiana University he has never repeated the same class twice in five years.

His advice for prospective teachers: "Try to read the class in a general sense, and respond to it, then structure the class accordingly. If you're a good teacher, you learn from the students. After all these years, I still say I hope I gave a good class."

LEFT: David Fernandez; From
the archives of David Fernandez

ABOVE: David Fernandez (with Joaquín De Luz)
From the archives of David Fernandez

RIGHT: Rose-Marie Menes
Photographer:
Marcia Rudy

LEFT: Donna Silva.
Donna with Munchkin, July 2016
From the archives of Donna Silva

LEFT: Laura Young
Photographer: Chris Mehil

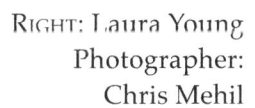

RIGHT: Laura Young
Photographer: Chris Mehil

ABOVE: Lois Bewley
New York City Ballet rehearsal of *The Figure in the Carpet* with George Balanchine and dancers (Leslie Ruchala behind him with Lois Bewley at right), choreography by George Balanchine (New York) 1960. ©NYPL
Photographer: Martha Swope

LEFT: Daniel Duell
Daniel Duell in Peter Martins' *Calcium Light Night*. 1978. ©NYPL
Photographer: Martha Swope

RIGHT: Darla Hoover
Photographer:
Rosalie O'Connor

LEFT: Louis Johnson
Louis Johnson in *Variations*, 1955.
©NYPL.
Photographer: Walter E. Owen

ABOVE: Peter Naumann with dancer Renee Estópinal
New York City Ballet production of *The Goldberg Variations* with Renee Estópinal and Peter Naumann, choreography by Jerome Robbins (New York) 1977. ©NYPL

LEFT: Nina Novak
Photographer: Maurice Seymour

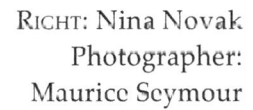

LEFT: Nina Novak
Photographer:
Maurice Seymour

RIGHT: Nina Novak
Photographer:
Maurice Seymour

LEFT: Nina Novak
Photographer:
Maurice Seymour

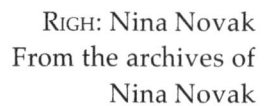

RIGH: Nina Novak
From the archives of
Nina Novak

ABOVE: Colleen Neary
Photographer: Martha Swope

BELOW: Delia Peters
production of Dances at a Gathering with Delia Peters, choreography by Jerome Robbins (New York) 1976. ©NYPL
Photographer: Martha Swope

ABOVE: Lawrence Rhodes teaching
Photographer: Rosalie O'Connor

ABOVE: Bruce Wells
Photographer: Jack Mitchell
Used with permission of Craig
Highberger, Executive Director of
Jack Mitchell Archives

RIGHT: Bruce Wells
From the archives of Bruce Wells

220 DANCE ON

Made in the USA
Middletown, DE
18 November 2020